ALSO BY
W. SCOTT MOORE

Dead Ends or Destiny?
*Seven Paths through the
Wilderness Experiences of Life*

Exit Wounds
Healing from the Hurts of the Ministry

Partners in Planting:
*Starting and Staffing a New Testament
Church*

Rural Pastor's Handbook:
A How to Guide for Leading Your Flock

Rural Revival:
*Growing Churches in Shrinking
Communities*

Supernatural Strategy:
*Discovering the Lost Key to Effective
Evangelism*

Uganda's Messianic Muslim:
*How Jesus Christ is Transforming
the Life and Ministry of Nassan Ibrahim*

THE GREATEST RURAL CHURCH IN AMERICA

How One Man's Vision Became
An Amazing Reality

W. Scott Moore

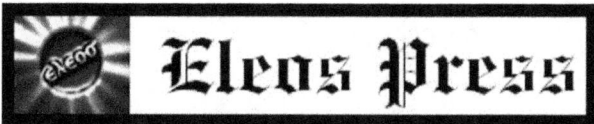

Eleos Press

Rogersville, AL

First Printing
The Greatest Rural Church in America

Author: W. Scott Moore, B.B.A., M. Div., D. Min.
© 2014 by Eleos Press www.eleospress.com

Cover Art: W. Scott Moore
Cover Design: W. Scott Moore
Interior Formatting: Eleos Press www.eleospress.com
Also available in eBook form

Unless otherwise noted, all "Scripture quotations taken from the New American Standard Bible®, Copyright © 1960, 1962, 1963, 1968, 1971, 1972, 1973, 1975, 1977, 1995 by The Lockman Foundation. Used by permission." (www.Lockman.org)

ISBN-13: 978-0692300084

TABLE OF CONTENTS

have known Bro. Jackie Shelton from the year 1984 until shortly before his passing in 2013. I can honestly say that I knew him when... I know a *lot* about Bro. Jackie, and most of it has been good.

If you are expecting some kind of exposé, a "tell-all" book, you will be greatly disappointed! Rather, this book is a tribute to a hero. The world certainly needs more of them — godly men and women that have proudly held high the standard of Jesus Christ. Jackie Shelton was, unquestionably, such a man.

This is a book about a man that I consider to be a spiritual "father." Bro. Jackie challenged me to work harder, to witness regularly, and to pray fervently. For that, I will always love and appreciate him.

Bro. Jackie and I may have been as different as night and day, but we worked extremely well together. The one complemented the other. King Solomon said it well:[1]

> *Two are better than one; because they have a good reward for their labour. For if they fall, the one will lift up his fellow: but woe to him that is alone when he falleth; for he hath not another to help him up. Again, if two lie together, then they have heat: but how can one be warm alone? And if one prevail against him, two shall withstand him; and a threefold cord is not quickly broken.*

I returned to work with Bro. Jackie in 1992, after having served as a mission pastor in Toledo, Ohio. However, this book focuses primarily on our first joint ministry — the years 1984 - 1987. I have chosen these years for several reasons:

---

[1] Ecclesiastes 4:9-12.

1. I was the most impressionable—I listened to every word that Bro. Jackie said.

2. Pleasant Grove Baptist Church was still small enough to enable Bro. Jackie to fully share his vision for the church with me.

3. Bro. Jackie often fondly referred to this period of time as "the Glory Days."

Over the years, I have heard preachers that were more polished than Bro. Jackie, but none that were any more faithful to the Word of God. I have also observed more accomplished soul-winners than Bro. Jackie, but I have never seen anyone who was more consistent.

But one thing is certain. I have *never* met another man as wise in the art of growing a rural church as Bro. Jackie.

Do these principles work? Are they transferrable? Can they be used effectively in your setting? The answer is, in the words of notable political figure, Sarah Palin, "You betcha!"

My family and I moved to Toledo, Ohio, in 1987 so that I could serve as the pastor of the King's Road Baptist Church. I knew exactly what I was getting into — a church that had split so many times that it had only three remaining members. And they were mad at *each other*!

I set out to be Jackie Shelton *junior* — a carbon copy of the pastor with whom I had served for the previous three years. I made a commitment to pray a lot. Although, I must confess, I did not arise quite as early in the morning as did Bro. Jackie. I tried for a few months, but kept falling asleep in the middle of my prayers.

I visited in the community like "nobody's business." Did it work? I believe that the facts speak for themselves. My wife, Diane, later told me, "During our five years in Ohio, we were able to reach more than 200 people with the Gospel!"

In those same five years, we baptized forty-two people into church membership.

We were able to increase our Sunday school attendance by approximately one hundred people.

We began a bus ministry, picking up fifteen to twenty children each Sunday morning, using the church van that was donated to us by the wonderful people of the Pleasant Grove Baptist Church. Two couples—Trillmon and Carolyn Steele and Onam and Louise Whitlow—delivered the van to us in Ohio.

We became the thirteenth-ranked church in per capita baptisms for the entire state of Ohio in 1989.

We were recognized as the number one ranked church in per capita financial support of the Cooperative Program in the state of Ohio in

1988, and the forty-ninth ranked church in that same category in1990.

Last, and *certainly* not least, we hosted a revival in 1991, during which forty-two people made professions of faith in the Lord Jesus Christ. We were a little disappointed — we had been praying for fifty! Not surprisingly, Jackie Shelton was our evangelist for the revival.

Use this book for the glory of God. Learn from Jackie Shelton — pastor of the "Greatest Rural Church in America." And remember — Jesus is Lord!

Your brother in the ministry,
W. Scott Moore

consider Jackie Shelton to be one of the most remarkable men of God I ever met. On a scale of 1-10 (with 10 being the best), I would rate him a 20!! I have seldom known any preacher who has impressed me more.

From the first revival I preached for him at Pleasant Grove until the last, my appreciation for him only increased. Unlike some we often meet in leadership roles, he was one of those rare individuals whom the more you knew about him the more you loved and admired him. And that probably explains why he could have such a long and fruitful ministry at that one church.

His record of church growth and evangelism at that rural congregation can only be explained by the touch of God's grace and anointing. And Jackie was one who keenly knew the absolute necessity of them both. He was humble enough to know he needed God - and wise enough not to attempt anything without Him!

When I came to Pleasant Grove for a revival, I knew before I arrived that it would be bathed in prayer and that every effort possible would be made to bring lost men and women, boys and girls, to the services. Some of the greatest meetings I have ever had were conducted at Pleasant Grove - and that says nothing about me - but everything about Brother Jackie and the passion he instilled into his church to reach the lost.

He was a dear, dear friend whom I greatly loved - and now greatly miss.

I am delighted that Scott Moore has chosen to write this book. For those of us who loved and admired Jackie so much, it will be a greatly loved treasure - a constant reminder of a man who touched us all in a unique and unforgettable way. And for those who never met or knew Jackie, it will be a rich blessing to read these insights into the life and ministry of a truly gifted man of God who so faithfully served the Lord in the place where he was assigned.

Evangelist Junior Hill
Hartselle, AL

INTRODUCTION

Long before the ready availability of books, people used the oral tradition in passing along their stories. A father or mother would tell stories to their children. In turn, the children would tell the stories to *their* children, and so on.

This book has its roots in the oral tradition. It is *oral history*—"a written work based on oral history."[2] I make no claims to having a foolproof memory. I do, however, distinctly remember the stories that Bro. Jackie has shared with me along the way—stories I

---

[2] MERRIAM-WEBSTER'S COLLEGIATE DICTIONARY AND THESAURUS, DELUXE AUDIO EDITION®, Version 2.5, Copyright © Merriam-Webster, Incorporated, 47 Federal Street, P.O. Box 28l, Springfield, MA 01102.

have gleaned from spending countless hours with him — driving to hospitals, meeting to discuss church needs, and just fellowshipping together. I have endeavored to share these stories with you.

I hope that you, like me, enjoy a little humor from time to time. If so, you should have a few laughs as you read the sections entitled, "On a Lighter Note."

I have also included several sections for the more thoughtful among you. These snippets are designated as "On a Serious Note."

Writing this book has been a massive undertaking. I have had to pick and choose. It has been somewhat like the Apostle John's description of the exploits of our Lord:

> *Jesus did many other things as well. If every one of them were written down, I suppose that*

even the whole world would not have room for the books that would be written.[3]

I will attempt to show you the "man behind the curtain" — the Wizard of Moulton, Alabama. If you *thought* you knew Bro. Jackie, you probably *didn't*. Fortunately, if you did not have the privilege of truly knowing Bro. Jackie, at the end of this book, you *will*!

Bro. Jackie's dream was to "write a book... and minister to rural churches to help them grow as he has seen Pleasant Grove grow."[4] My prayer is that this book will become the fulfillment of that dream.

---

[3] John 21:25.
[4] "Wren Pastor Retires after 23 Growing Years." The Alabama Baptist. 24 June 2004.

WHO HE WAS[5]

Jackie Shelton was born on November 21, 1938. He came from good stock. His father, Ernest Shelton, served for many years as the circuit clerk. I never had the privilege of meeting his dad.

My wife, Diane, and I became acquainted with Bro. Jackie's mother, "Miss Hilda" Elkins Shelton, when we had the occasional privilege of driving her home after church services.

She was one of the sweetest ladies I have ever known. In her younger years:

---

[5] Taken from http://www.obitsforlife.com/ obituary685298/Shelton--Jackie-.php, site visited on 2/18/2014.

Mrs. Shelton's kindness and helpful attitude made her a favorite among the thousands of visitors at the courthouse during her 22 years of service there. She worked in the Circuit Clerk's office with her husband, the late Ernest Shelton, who served 30 years as circuit clerk. She and her husband retired together in 1976.[6]

Bro. Jackie graduated from the Lawrence County High School in Moulton, Alabama. He attended Auburn University for two years, before transferring to the University of Alabama. He graduated from that institution in 1962. He subsequently did post-graduate work at "Ole Miss," the University of Mississippi.

Bro. Jackie was a part owner of the Sivley Cotton Company in Hartselle, Alabama. Having received his call to enter into the ministry, he left that business in 1976 to attend the New Orleans

---

[6]

http://www.obitsforlife.com/obituary/617850/Shelton-Hilda.php, site visited on 3/5/2014.

Baptist Theological Seminary. He graduated with a Master of Divinity degree.

Bro. Jackie was the pastor of only two churches. He served for four-and-one-half years at his first church, the Steep Hollow Baptist Church in Poplarville, Mississippi. He completed his additional twenty-four-and-one-half years of ministry at the Pleasant Grove Baptist Church in Moulton, Alabama.

Bro. Jackie was a devoted family man. He is survived by Ben-Ann Shelton, his wife of 51 years, their three sons, Stuart, Brett, and Ben, six grandchildren, and two great-grandchildren. At the time of his passing, he was also survived by one brother and two sisters.

Additionally, he is survived by hundreds, if not thousands, of spiritual children—the men and women, boys and girls that he led to saving faith in our Lord Jesus Christ.

W. Scott Moore

Jackie's Life before His Call

Bro. Jackie could honestly, and proudly, say that he had never, at any time, tasted alcohol. In fact, in his younger days he had one vice, and only one—playing pool at the local pool hall.

He would finish his college classes for the day and head to the pool room. He would offer to take on all comers. As many of the losers would now testify, he was, apparently, quite good.

As a former pool playing pastor, Bro. Jackie was in good company. Johnny Hunt,[7] pastor of First Baptist Church in Woodstock, Georgia, and Dusty McLemore,[8] pastor of

---

[7] Johnny M. Hunt. <u>Building Your Leadership Résumé: Developing the Legacy that Will Outlast You</u> (Nashville: Broadman and Holman Publishing Group, 2003).

[8] Dusty is completing his first book this year. I am the editor. It will be entitled: Dusty McLemore. <u>Gambling</u>

Lindsey Lane Baptist Church in Athens, Alabama, also misspent their youths in various pool parlors.

On a Lighter Note

Those who were acquainted with Bro. Jackie knew him to be a very serious-minded man of God. He also had his "human" side.

His daily lunchtime meal consisted of a Pepsi Cola™ and a double pack of Reese's Peanut Butter Cups™. While attending classes at Auburn University, he discovered that none of the local stores sold Pepsi Cola™. He was told that Auburn was "Coca-Cola™ country."

He concocted a scheme. First, he went to the local convenience store to ask for a Pepsi. Not surprisingly, he was told that they did not.

A couple of days later, he sent a friend to the same store with the same question. The

---

with Eternity: The Loser Wins (Athens, AL: LLBC Publishing, 2014).

friend stood for several moments in front of the soft drink section of the cooler. He walked up to the counter with a bewildered look on his face. He asked, "Where is your Pepsi™?" The clerk responded, "We don't have any. Why don't you just buy a Coke?" The friend, as per Bro. Jackie's instruction, just shook his head as he walked slowly out of the store.

Two more days passed. A second friend went into the same store and asked the same question. He received the same response.

Bro. Jackie said, "Within two weeks, that store had stocked up on Pepsi™." "And," he said with a grin and a twinkle in his eye, "Now everybody in the town of Auburn sells Pepsi™!"

Another Lighter Note

He also told me the story about his early days of playing golf. He and another man had completed 17 holes, and were about to play the 18th. The two men agreed to place a relatively innocent wager on the longest drive. They agreed that, when they arrived at the clubhouse, the man with the shorter drive would buy a Pepsi™ for the man with the longer drive. There was only one stipulation—you had to be able to find your ball.

The other man was the first to play off of the tee. He hit a fairly good ball, but Bro. Jackie knew he could beat it. And he did. He drove his ball way past the other man's.

But Bro. Jackie had a problem. Although the other man's ball had stopped short of his ball, Bro. Jackie couldn't find his. He and the other man searched and searched, but to no avail.

Finally, Bro. Jackie reached into his pocket and drew out another ball. He dropped it on the ground. He stooped down, picked it up, and proclaimed, "Here it is."

The other man replied, "That's not your ball."

Bro. Jackie snapped, "And how do you know that?"

The man reached into *his* pocket, pulled out a ball, held it up, and said, "Because I've got *your* ball right here!"

Jackie's First Church

Bro. Jackie made a visit to the placement office at the New Orleans Baptist Theological Seminary. He asked about the availability of a place where he could preach. He was informed that no churches were currently available, but that his name would be added to a list. He would be notified when, and if, an opportunity should arise.

A few days later, he received a phone call. A little church in the area, Steep Hollow Baptist

Church in Poplarville, Mississippi, needed someone to supply for them on Sunday.

Poplarville, "home of the annual Blueberry Jubilee,"[9] is located in Pearl River County. The town of Poplarville has been classified as "100% rural." In 2012, it had a population of only 2,834. Sixty-two-and-four tenths percent of the population was affiliated with churches in the Southern Baptist Convention.[10]

Bro. Jackie gladly accepted their invitation. And, a few weeks later, they invited him back. Eventually, they called him to be their pastor. This was unheard of—a first-year student receiving a church—when so many of the upper classmen were still waiting in line. But God had promised Jackie that He would not

---

[9] http://www.poplarville.net, site visited on 2/19/2014.

[10] http://www.city-data.com/city/Poplarville-Mississippi.html, site visited on 2/19/2014/

fail him, and that He would provide for his needs.

Did the church grow? Apparently so. During Bro. Jackie's tenure as pastor, "Steep Hollow… [Baptist Church went] from 80 in Sunday school to a high attendance of 365."[11]

The Pastors' Conference

Bro. Jackie made his first visit to the Pearl River Baptist Association to attend the weekly pastors' conference. He listened to the pastors of the larger churches as they boasted about their attendance and their offerings on the previous Sunday morning.

After the conference had ended, one of these pastors approached Bro. Jackie. The man extended his hand. He introduced himself. He asked Bro. Jackie, "Are you new here?"

---

[11] "Wren Pastor Retires." The Alabama Baptist.

Bro. Jackie replied in the affirmative. He then said, "I am the new pastor of the Steep Hollow Baptist Church."

Apparently, the man was unimpressed. Surrounded by his peers, he began to smile broadly. He and his fellow "First Baptist pastors" began to laugh. He sneered, "Steep Hollow? Why would anyone want to pastor a church like *that*?"

Bro. Jackie was deeply wounded by the man's statement. In response, he made a vow: "I will *never* boast about what is happening in my church. I will *never* do to someone else what this man has done to me." And, as far as I know, he never did.

For instance, Bro. Jackie invited Junior Hill to preach during our week of revival in 1996.[12] At the end of the meetings, I was given

---

[12] See Appendix B. The baptisms that resulted from this revival were added to the Annual Church Profile for the 1997 church year.

the privilege of personally baptizing the more than 60 men and women, boys and girls that had given their lives to Jesus Christ. Consequently, the baptisms completely preempted the Sunday evening service.

On a Lighter Note

Most of the preachers that I know have a set of waders hanging in the entryway to their baptistries. Not Bro. Jackie. His nickname for waders was "cheaters." He insisted that he, and anyone else that performed the baptisms at Pleasant Grove, get wet with the baptismal candidates.

His reasoning for refusing to use "cheaters" may have pointed back to his insistence that he would never ask anyone else to do what he himself was unwilling to do. It also motivated him to check the temperature of the water. If the water had been too hot, he also would have been burned; if the water had been

12

too cold, he would have shivered along with the candidates.

Bro. Jackie's Remarks

The morning after we had baptized 60 people, Bro. Jackie attended the pastors' conference at the Muscle Shoals Baptist Association in Moulton, Alabama,. A fellow pastor loudly proclaimed, "Jackie, I hear you had real revival at Pleasant Grove last week."

Bro. Jackie's simple, understated response was, "God is good." When pressed by others for more information, Bro. Jackie simply repeated his previous statement, "God is good."

<u>Their Faith</u>

Bro. Jackie often spoke about the simple, child-like faith of the members of the Steep Hollow Baptist Church. They, like the four friends in the following story that brought the paralytic to Jesus, unreservedly trusted in the Lord:

> *And it came to pass on a certain day, as he was teaching, that there were Pharisees and doctors of the law sitting by, which were come out of every town of Galilee, and Judaea, and Jerusalem: and the power of the Lord was present to heal them. And, behold, men brought in a bed a man which was taken with a palsy: and they sought means to bring him in, and to lay him before him. And when they could not find by what way they might bring him in because of the multitude, they went upon the housetop, and let him down through the tiling with his couch into the midst before Jesus. And when he saw their faith, he said unto him, Man, thy sins are forgiven thee.*[13]

That last sentence fragment is the key: "when he saw *their* [emphasis mine] faith." In Bro. Jackie's words, "They [the members of Steep Hollow Baptist Church] believed God." When one of them would get sick, he said, "They were convinced that God was going to

---

[13] Luke 5:17-20.

heal them." "And," he concluded, "Do you know what? God *did!*" Bro. Jackie saw many healed because of their belief.

On a Lighter Note

One Sunday, the members of a needy family joined the Steep Hollow Baptist Church. They were faithful attenders, coming to the church "every time the doors were opened." The father worked long hours, in an effort to provide for the needs of his family. He only had one problem: he didn't have any means of transportation. He and his family members were forced to walk everywhere that they went.

Bro. Jackie asked the church members to meet the family's need. They voted to purchase an old pickup truck for this family. The father was so excited, and they were all grateful.

But then it happened. The family's attendance at church became sporadic. And then they stopped coming altogether.

15

One Sunday morning, as he was walking into the church, Bro. Jackie heard the loud honking of a car horn. Someone was calling his name. He looked toward the highway. There it was — the truck! All of the members of the family were hanging out of the windows and out of the truck bed, waving at him. The fishing poles told the rest of the story — they wouldn't be coming to church *this* Sunday, either!

Jackie Comes to Pleasant Grove

His Hesitation

Bro. Jackie was approached by the pulpit committee from the Pleasant Grove Baptist Church, sometime around 1980. His first impression was, "No!" He remembered his days as a deacon at Moulton Baptist Church. He had observed, first-hand, the difficulties that various pastors had encountered at the "city" church. As a result, he did not feel that was his calling.

So, needless to say, Bro. Jackie was hesitant to return to his hometown. But he was later quoted as saying, "I fasted and prayed and knew this was where I was supposed to go."[14] Those were not just words — Bro. Jackie's life was continually punctuated by prayer.

His Acceptance of the Call

So why did he return? Why did he accept the call? It certainly wasn't because he needed to leave Steep Hollow. He loved the people from that church, and they loved him. He spoke of them often.

Bro. Jackie made the decision to return to Moulton, Alabama, because of prayer. Prayer and a vision.

---

[14] "Wren Pastor Retires." The Alabama Baptist.

He sought the Lord earnestly before making his decision. As he prayed, he received his vision for Lawrence County, Alabama — to build "the greatest rural church in America."

He had some distinct advantages. Although the people of Moulton knew a lot about *him*, he also knew a lot about *them*. He knew their thoughts. He knew what their reactions would be. He knew their resistance to change. He knew what he *could* and *couldn't* do.

HIS SECRETS FOR GROWTH

Bro. Jackie's secrets for growth can be divided into four broad categories: his convictions, his techniques, his programs, and his events.

His Convictions

Bro. Jackie was a man of many convictions. He believed strongly in prayer, hard work, the Bible, the Lord's Day, and maintaining the proper image in the Moulton community.

Prayer

Bro. Jackie was committed to his own personal spiritual growth. Many factors in his life contributed to that goal. The activity that would become his spiritual trademark was his unequaled prayer life.

To say that Bro. Jackie was a *driven* man would be an understatement! He was, without a doubt, the hardest working man that I have ever met. His day began at 4:00 in the morning. He frequently stated, "The sun has never risen over Moulton, Alabama, that I wasn't already up and praying."

On a Lighter Note

Dr. David Skinner, Professor Emeritus of Hebrew and Old Testament at the Mid-America Baptist Theological Seminary in Cordova, Tennessee, was reared in Lexington, Mississippi.[15] Before working at the seminary, Dr. Skinner was also a "country" preacher.

---

[15] http://www.mabts.edu/academics/get-know-our-faculty/faculty-bios/dr-david-skinner, site visited on 2/25/2014.

He related the following story to a group of us students: "As a pastor, I made a habit of getting up early in the morning to pray and study my Bible. That was the best part of the day — and it was quiet."

"My telephone rang one morning, at around 5:00. A farmer (one of my church members), was on the other end of the line. His first words were, 'Pastor, did I wake you up?' Since I had been up for more than an hour, I could honestly say, 'No, brother, you didn't.'"

Dr. Skinner continued, "I thought about what he had asked me. You see, in a rural community, *everybody* gets up early in the morning. They have to! The best time to work on a farm is before the sun comes up."

"Farmers tend to think that pastors are lazy. 'Most pastors,' they think, 'are just city folk. They like to lie around in the bed until

8:00. They are just lazy! But they can't help it. That's how city folks are.'"

"So I plotted my revenge. I waited a few weeks. And then I called the farmer back—at *4:00* in the morning. The phone rang several times before he finally picked it up. Sleepily, he answered, 'Hello?'"

"Cheerfully, I responded, 'Oh, I'm sorry brother. Did I wake *you* up?'"

Hard Work

Motivational speaker John C. Maxwell has coined the term, "the Law of the Lid." Maxwell explained:[16]

> *Leadership ability is the lid that determines a person's level of effectiveness. The lower an individual's ability to lead, the lower the lid on his potential. The higher the individual's ability to lead, the higher the lid on his potential. "*

---

[16] http://www.johnmaxwell.com/blog/the-law-of-the-lid, site visited on 2/20/2014.

In other words, the growth of the organization—in this case, the church—will either be limited or augmented by the capabilities of its leader.

Bro. Jackie never asked anyone to do what he himself was unwilling to do. In fact, he raised his personal "bar" so high that he didn't expect anyone else to attempt to measure up.

After praying, on a typical day Bro. Jackie would visit the hospitals. He would begin by going to the Cracker Barrel Restaurant™ just north of the UAB Hospital in Birmingham, Alabama—a one-way trip of nearly 85 miles. He liked going to the Cracker Barrel™ because they would open their doors 30 minutes early, just for him. They would serve him coffee, juice, and a single biscuit (since two biscuits would have been too many).

After completing his visits in Birmingham, he would proceed to the Huntsville Hospital in Huntsville, Alabama—an additional 95 miles. He would complete his journey by making a 50-mile return trip by way of the hospital in Decatur, Alabama, through the hospital in Moulton, Alabama, and then back to the church. His morning completed, Bro. Jackie would then start making his local visits.

Why did he work so hard? Bro. Jackie once told me, "I have seen a lot of pastors come and go throughout the years. Most of them want to come in and just 'coast' for the first couple of years. The problem with that mentality is that they develop a reputation in the community for being lazy. When they sense that the people feel that way about them, they will start working. But, no matter how hard they try, they will be unable to shake the label."

On a Serious Note

Bro. Jackie not only *understood* the characteristics of the rural community, he had also personally *adopted* them. He once told me a story about the pastor that had followed him at Steep Hollow Baptist Church.

He said, "The man has his doctorate, so he is obviously very smart.[17] But he *never* visits! He doesn't understand how to grow a church like Steep Hollow. He thinks his job is to teach the *people* to make the visits. That won't work. He needs to get out of the office and into the community. He's going to kill that church!"[18]

Note: Bro. Jackie believed that, although equipping the saints to make the visits may be *scriptural* (Ephesians 4:11-12), it does not work in a rural church. The successful rural pastor, as Bro. Jackie saw it, must first demonstrate his willingness to carry the load *by himself.* Period.

---

[17] Rural folks are not particularly impressed with educational achievements.

[18] Reminiscent of Ecclesiastes 2:17-21.

The Bible

Bro. Jackie was a student of the Bible. At a pastors' and wives' Christmas banquet held by the Muscle Shoals Baptist Association, the pastors were challenged to write down the names of all of the books of the Bible. Those that could do it would receive a prize.

Several pastors took the pieces of paper given to them by then Director of Missions, Elmer Fowler. They wrote, "All of the books of the Bible." Bro. Fowler acknowledged their cleverness, and rewarded each of them with a prize.

One pastor, and *only* one, took the time to start with Genesis, end in Revelation, and write all 66 books of the Bible—in order. Would you like to guess his name? Jackie Shelton.

Bro. Jackie believed the Bible to be God's Word. For him, it was literally true. He never questioned the veracity of the Scriptures.

28

Because of this commitment to the Bible, and after he had been called to preach, he made plans to attend the Mid-America Baptist Theological Seminary.

Dr. Phil Allison, vice-president of the seminary, had previously served as Bro. Jackie's pastor at Moulton Baptist Church. Bro. Jackie had also heard the president of Mid-America Baptist Theological Seminary,[19] Dr. Gray Allison (Phil's brother), speak during many revival meetings at the church. He knew that Dr. Gray and Dr. Phil both had a passion for reaching the unsaved, a passion that he shared.

It was, therefore, no surprise that, after surrendering to the call to the ministry, Bro. Jackie fully intended to enroll at Mid-America. He has always loved the Mid-America Baptist Theological Seminary. In fact, he supported the

---

[19] My alma mater.

seminary financially, to the extent that he was asked to be a member of the Advisory Board.

He made an appointment with Dr. Gray to tour the campus. When he arrived at the seminary, he was informed that Dr. Gray had been called away on business. Another professor escorted him through the facilities. He returned home, and began a season of prayer regarding his seminary education.

Bro. Jackie and his family members were led subsequently in another direction — to attend the New Orleans Baptist Theological Seminary in Louisiana. Bro. Jackie, conservative in his theology, knew that he would be going to a seminary in which many of the professors held a liberal view of the Bible. But he also knew that he was personally "grounded" well enough to handle it.

Jackie Shelton
Which Version?

Adrian Rogers, pastor of the Bellevue Baptist Church in Cordova, Tennessee, once remarked:

> *My daughter has started reading a different translation of the Bible — the New International Version. She said, "Daddy, did you know that when you read from the King James Bible, and then tell us what it means, you are basically saying what it says in the New International Version?"*
>
> *I replied, "I'm not surprised."*
>
> *She then asked, "Then why don't you just preach from the New International Version?"*
>
> *I answered, "I guess that I have just been preaching from the King James for too long. All of the verses in my sermon notes are from the King James Version, and all of the Bible verses that I have memorized are from the King James Version. So, honey, I think I will just have to keep using it."*

Likely, and for similar reasons, Bro. Jackie had also made the same decision. He taught and preached exclusively from the King James Bible, with one minor distinction — he preferred the

31

New Scofield Reference Bible. He frequently explained to any potential detractors that the New Scofield Reference Bible had made only a few *minor, insignificant* changes to the King James Version—instead of "devils," the word was "demons." As Bro. Jackie pointed out, "There is only *one* devil. There are *many* demons."

Bro. Jackie and I discussed his decision to preach from the King James Version. He said, looking back upon his days as a deacon at Moulton Baptist Church, "I remember when one of our pastors decided to change the pew Bibles[20] to the New International Version. His action only caused a *mild* ripple among the members, but it was a ripple nonetheless."[21]

---

[20] Bibles placed in the pew rack for the use of those people that either did not have, or did not bring, a Bible to church.

[21] For Bro. Jackie, the "ripple" had been an unnecessary battle that he had decided to avoid.

Bro. Jackie continued, "I know there are many fine translations out there. But I don't think the attempt to change the version in a rural Baptist church is a very good idea."

Chapel Hour

Bro. Jackie was delighted when Dr. W. A. Criswell of First Baptist Church in Dallas, TX, was invited to speak during the weekly chapel hour at the seminary. As he preached, Dr. Criswell stepped down from the platform. He held his Bible up conspicuously in front of him. He walked up to the section of seats reserved for the professors. He shook his Bible in their faces. He shouted, "This is a Bible! It is God's holy Word!" And then he taunted them with the question, "Can't you highly educated men understand that?"

The Lord's Day

When I first heard Bro. Jackie speak about the topic of Sundays, I thought that he must have been from another century. I was wrong. He was not from another *century* — he was from another *culture*. Whereas I had grown up in Atlanta, Georgia, a place where every business was open 24 hours a day, seven days a week, Bro. Jackie had not. He remembered how things used to be. He believed, and rightfully so, that the members of his rural church should agree with him. As a result, the members of Pleasant Grove both understood and reluctantly endorsed his message.

He made it abundantly clear to all of us that we should "remember the Sabbath day, to keep it holy."[22] In fact, on more than one occasion, he said, "I don't buy anything from businesses on Sundays, and you shouldn't,

_____

[22] Exodus 20:8.

either. If you need gas, buy it on Saturday. If you need groceries, either buy them on Saturday or wait until Monday."

He continued, "If you want to go out to eat, don't do it on Sunday. How, in the world, are we going to get people to come to church if you are the cause of them having to work? If we will stop supporting these businesses on Sundays, maybe they will close for the day. And then their employees will be able to come to church."

His Image

"Image" includes everything that a person does to improve how people see them and, ultimately, whether or not they will respect them. As a rural pastor, with roots in the community, Bro. Jackie believed in the importance of maintaining his personal appearance. For instance:

1. He never had a hair out of place.

2. He shaved twice daily to avoid the dreaded "five-o'clock shadow."

3. He was always well-dressed. Most of the time, he would be wearing a suit. His idea of "casual" was a dress shirt, a tie, khakis, and a sport coat.[23]

4. Every week, he would take his 100% cotton shirts[24] to the Culver Cleaners on his way to visit church members in the hospital in the old section of Decatur, Alabama. He would have them laundered, highly starched, and pressed.

5. He had a self-assigned parking space near the church offices. Although

---

[23] His idea of "getting comfortable" was to remove his jacket while sitting at his desk. What about the tie? He kept it on.

[24] He told me that most pastors would not like the thickness and weight of a pure cotton shirt. For him, it was a carryover from, and a reminder of, his days as a trader in the cotton business.

there was no "Reserved for Pastor" sign, we all knew that it was *his* place.

6. Although he frequently traveled on the dirt roads of north Alabama (in rural Alabama, a.k.a., "rock" roads), he:

    a. Kept his shoes shined.

    b. Kept his car in immaculate condition, both inside and out.[25]

7. Bro. Jackie, unlike me, also kept an extremely neat desk.

On a Lighter Note

Bro. Jackie had, obviously, put in a lot of effort in creating and sustaining the proper image. This would be clearly demonstrated by

---

[25] Bro. Jackie came to church one Wednesday night and, as they say, he was "fit to be tied!" He told us that he had just finished washing his car when, suddenly, a "demon possessed bird" flew over. Bro. Jackie knew that Satan must have sent the bird, because the bird had targeted his car with its droppings!

an incident involving filling the baptistry with water.

Bro. Jackie, though tall in spirit, was short in stature. One day, as was his custom, he had climbed onto the seat of the back pew in the choir loft to turn off the water to the baptistry.

Having completed his task, he turned around with the intention of stepping down from the pew. Sadly, he lost his footing. Down he went, hitting the pew in front of him. He either bruised or cracked a rib.

The word of Bro. Jackie's mishap traveled quickly. Always the jokester, fellow pastor Ted Vafeas asked me for a picture of Bro. Jackie. He said, "I have a cousin that draws caricatures for his local newspaper. I think we can have some fun with this."

I gave him the picture. A few weeks later, Ted handed the sketch to me. In the picture, Bro. Jackie was wearing a cape. The letter "S" was emblazoned on the front of his superhero's costume. He was walking *through* a set of splintering pews as they crumbled before him. He had become "Super Jackie!"

I measured the borders of the canvass, and built a custom frame to fit it. I presented the picture to Bro. Jackie. He didn't laugh. He didn't even smile. Although I had fully expected him to hang the picture in his office, I never saw it again.

Years later, I asked Bro. Jackie what had happened to the picture. He curtly replied, "I don't know where it is."

I think that I know. I believe that it is either buried in the back yard of the parsonage or resting peacefully underneath several tons of other "masterpieces" in the Lawrence County Sanitary Landfill in Moulton, Alabama.

His Self-Control

Bro. Jackie was an extremely disciplined man. His prayer life and his work ethic were beyond reproach. Bro. Jackie started out his day with what he called a "big breakfast" — basically, one biscuit and a cup of coffee. His lunch fare, as I have already mentioned, was always the same — a can of Pepsi Cola™ and a double pack of Reese's Peanut Butter Cups™. As a result, he remained trim throughout his ministry and into his retirement.

His Events

Events may be defined as those occasional undertakings that have the potential for producing instantaneous growth. However, events should supplement, rather than replace, hard work and the ongoing programs of a rural church.

<u>Revivals</u>

Revival truly took place shortly after Bro. Jackie's arrival at Pleasant Grove in 1980. He invited a pastor friend from southern Mississippi, James Hickman (better known to us as *Brother* Hickman), to preach for him. One of Bro. Hickman's revival messages has literally changed the destiny of Pleasant Grove Baptist Church.

At the beginning of this unforgettable service, Brother Hickman wound up an alarm clock. Unbeknownst to the congregation, he had secretly set the alarm to go off at 12:00 noon. He told the people, "I want you to imagine that every minute that passes on this clock is one year. There are thirty years left—thirty years before Jesus Christ comes back. When the hands of the clock reach 12:00 noon, He will return."

Bro. Hickman didn't tell the people that he had set the alarm to go off at 12:00. He

41

continued to preach. He updated the people by saying, "Now Jesus will be back in twenty years."

In Bro. Hickman's sermon, twenty years would become ten. Ten would become five. Suddenly, as Bro. Hickman started his invitation, the alarm sounded — and it sounded *loudly*.

Bro. Jackie later told me that masses of people began *running* down the aisle, desperately wanting to be saved. Teachers, deacons, and other church leaders realized that they had been lost. They were literally begging the Lord to save them. This event would mark the beginning of a new direction for Pleasant Grove Baptist Church.

Bro. Jackie reflected on the "Brother Hickman" revival in an interview, shortly before his retirement in 2004. He said:

> *I'll never forget it. It was the type of revival where, before you gave the invitation, people*

were just waiting to come. Some were even saved before services. It was just the Holy Spirit at work, and it was a real turning point. [26]

Subsequent Revivals

Rural churches will typically hold two revival meetings per year — one in the spring and the other in the fall. Pleasant Grove was no exception.

Pleasant Grove was no exception, that is, until Bro. Jackie became the pastor. Bro. Jackie believed in "bucking the system." He did not believe in having "revival for revival's sake." He told me, "We never have a revival just because we have always done it that way before."

His strategy was to wait until several people began to ask, "When is our next

---

[26] **Error! Main Document Only.**"Wren Pastor Retires." The Alabama Baptist.

revival?"[27]   When, in his estimation, enough people had been clamoring for revival that he believed they were becoming serious about it *then* he would schedule one.

Throughout the years, Bro. Jackie invited several other evangelists to preach at Pleasant Grove. His list included such notable figures as Dr. Gene Williams, president emeritus of the Luther Rice Seminary in Atlanta, Georgia, and Zach Terry, pastor of the Capshaw Baptist Church in Capshaw, Alabama.

But by far his favorite evangelist, and the most successful, was Junior Hill. Bro. Junior held five series revival meetings at Pleasant Grove Baptist Church during Bro. Jackie's 24-year tenure as pastor.

Bro. Junior is a singularly anointed man of God. His preaching has produced some

---

[27] Reminiscent of Bro. Jackie's antics in the "Pepsi at Auburn" story, pg. 5.

amazing results. (See Appendix C and the graph below)

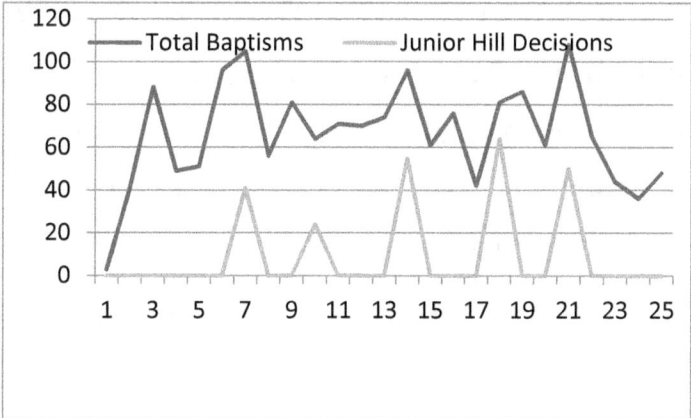

I am calling this phenomenon the "Junior Hill Effect." As you can see, Junior preached the revival services at Pleasant Grove during the two remarkable years in which more than 100 people were baptized (1986 and 2000).

His Programs

Programs are the ongoing activities that produce the incremental and sustainable growth in a rural church.

Evangelism

Dr. Gray Allison, President Emeritus of the Mid-America Baptist Theological Seminary in Cordova, Tennessee, often said, "If you give me an insurance salesman, I will give you a soul-winner." I believe Dr. Gray made this statement based upon three facts:

1. His personal experience — if memory serves, Dr. Gray had previously sold insurance.

2. Insurance agents are trained to sell an "intangible" product — something that you can neither see nor feel

3. Insurance agents are capable of handling rejection — they are accustomed to hearing more "noes" than "yeses."

Bro. Jackie certainly fit the bill. In addition to having worked at several other jobs prior to becoming a pastor, Bro. Jackie had also been a very successful agent with the Horace Mann Educators Corporation.[28]

Bro. Jackie's greatest passion was in reaching the unsaved with the Gospel of Jesus Christ. Every van bought, every building built, every mile traveled was for the purpose of reaching people for the Lord.

Bro. Jackie was never satisfied. When one person would accept Christ, he would ask them for referrals. He would say, "Is there anyone else in this house that needs Jesus?" If they said, "Yes," he would ask to speak with the others.

Satisfied that he had witnessed to everyone in the home, he would *then* inquire, "Do you have any relatives or friends in the Moulton area that I could talk to?" And he would be on his merry way, driving directly to the next house to share with the folks there the

---

[28] An insurance company specializing in coverage for teachers.

recent developments at the previous house. He would then give them the opportunity of making similar decisions for Christ.

His hard work definitely paid off. In his 24 years at Pleasant Grove, he baptized a total of 1,653 men and women, boys and girls for the glory of his Lord, Jesus Christ! (See the graph below and Appendix B)

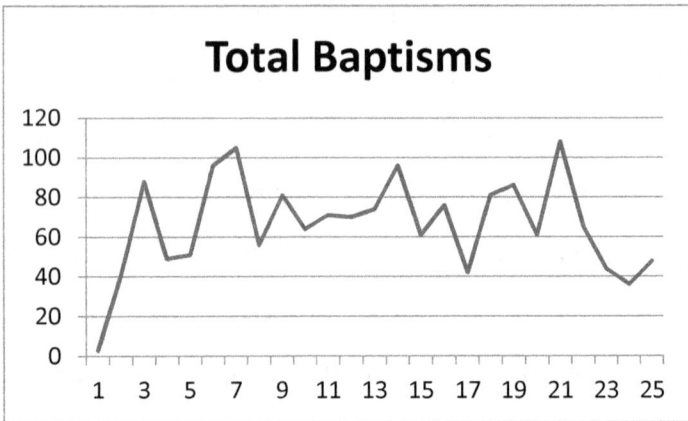

Total Baptisms

A Side Benefit

You are likely familiar with the story of the Philippian jailer the jailer in Acts 16:30. The man cried out to Paul and Silas, "Sirs, what must I do to be saved?"

You may not have personally experienced a similar encounter. But Bro. Jackie has, and on more than one occasion.

Why did Bro. Jackie personally experience the "Philippian Jailer" phenomenon? The answer is akin to a prevailing remark about Calvinism. "It is amazing how many of 'the *Elect*' you will meet when you are out regularly sharing your faith."

Over the years, Bro. Jackie was out regularly sharing his faith. He had, therefore, become an established and well-known soul-winner in the Moulton area. Consequently, people began seeking him out.

Barbara Jetton

The men from Pleasant Grove had adopted the home of a family in Grayson, Alabama, as a work project. The home had no running water and no inside bathroom. Our men had torn out and replaced the floors, run plumbing lines, added fixtures and, voilà, instant bathroom.

Eric Frost, a church member and maintenance supervisor from a local hospital, and I made a return trip to the home to put the finishing touches on the project. The family's matriarch, Barbara Jetton, placed a folding chair just outside the bathroom door so that she could watch us as we worked. Actually, she didn't *watch* us—she *glared* at us.

When we had completed the job and had safely returned to the car, Eric commented, "That woman scares me!" I didn't admit it at the time, but I totally agreed with him.

Barbara Jetton was the toughest mountain woman that you would ever not want to meet. That is, until something happened several weeks later.

Jackie Shelton

One particular day, I heard a knock. I opened the door. There she was, standing right in front of me—Barbara Jetton!

I stepped out of the doorway and onto the porch to talk with her. She led me out into the parking lot. She was obviously in distress.

I asked, "May I help you?"

She said, in an extremely breathy voice, "I need to see Bro. Jackie."

I explained, "He's not here. He is out of town. What can I do for you?"

She said, "You can't do anything for me. I have to see Bro. Jackie! I need to see him right now!"

We continued our conversation for a few minutes before she finally understood that Bro. Jackie was unavailable. She finally confided, "I need to be saved today. I know this will be my last chance. I have to be saved today, or I know that I will go to Hell. I can't wait any longer."

51

At that moment, I felt compelled to place my hand on her shoulder (Barbara would later tell me that she felt immediately at peace). I said, "Barbara, *I* can tell you how to be saved."

She said, "Okay."

I shared the Gospel with her, using the Romans Road plan of salvation.[29] She prayed the "Sinner's Prayer"[30] right there in the parking lot of Pleasant Grove Baptist Church.

Years later, Barbara lapsed into a lifestyle of flagrant immorality. Eventually, she fell back under conviction. She either had not truly been saved in the parking lot that day, or felt that she had somehow "lost her salvation."[31] For whatever reason, she once again found herself in

---

[29] Romans 3:23, 6:23, 5:8, 10:9, 10:10, and 10:13.

[30] Barbara admitted that she had a time in his life when she had disobeyed God. She also recognized the fact that her sins had separated her from God. She wanted to begin a relationship with God, so she asked Him to forgive her for her sins, to come into her life, and to give her eternal life through Jesus Christ.

[31] A theological impossibility (see John 10:28).

search of Bro. Jackie. He told her, once again, about Jesus. She prayed, once again, to be saved.

The point of the story is—whom did Barbara want to see when she wanted to be saved? Who immediately came to her mind? Whom did she associate with the Gospel? The obvious answer is *Jackie Shelton*.

A few more years had passed. Barbara died. The family members asked Bro. Jackie to perform her funeral service. Bro. Jackie asked them to allow me to assist him with the funeral, and they agreed. The two of us ministered together to her family.

The mother

Late one night, the mother of a couple of kids that rode one of our vans to church was taken to the hospital. She was in critical condition, she was dying, and she knew it.

The doctors and nurses in the Emergency Room had tried to sedate her, but nothing they had attempted was working. They had strapped her to a bed, but she continued to struggle. She kept screaming, "Bro. Jackie! Somebody please find Bro. Jackie!"

One of the nurses knew that the woman was referring to Jackie Shelton. She excused herself from the room. She placed a quick phone call to Bro. Jackie.

Bro. Jackie dressed quickly and drove to the hospital. He ran to the nurses' station. He was directed to one of the cubicles.

He asked the woman, "What's wrong?"

She said, "I'm dying, and I need to be saved."

Bro. Jackie knew that the woman had previously stolen a watch from one of our church members. He later told me, "I started to see if she was serious about being saved by asking her to tell me about the watch. But I didn't."

Bro. Jackie talked with her about sin. He explained to her the need for repentance. He told her that Jesus had died on the cross so that she might be saved, and that He was now alive and praying for her right at that moment.

He asked her if she would like to be saved. She said that she would. And she did.

She immediately became calm. Her contorted muscles began to relax. And then she died. Not as an unsaved sinner on her way to Hell, but rather as a new believer in Christ on her way to Heaven.

On a Lighter Note

Barbara Jetton's ex-husband, Pete Jetton, was known at Pleasant Grove as a "repeat offender." He was a member of the elite group that would come to the altar on a regular basis during invitations. He wanted to be saved—again and again and again.

This time, Bro. Jackie was ready for him. Pete, wearing his most contrite expression, told Bro. Jackie, "I need to be saved."

Bro. Jackie said, "No, Pete, you don't. Go back to your seat."

Pete pleaded, "*Please*, Bro. Jackie, I want to be saved!"

Bro. Jackie replied, "No, Pete. You're not serious about this. You are just playing games with God. Go back to your seat."

After several more exchanges, Bro. Jackie relented. He led Pete to the Lord "one more time."

The day of Pete's baptism finally arrived. Bro. Jackie had already baptized a couple of other candidates. Pete had joined him in the baptistry. Bro. Jackie said, "I baptize you, Pete Jetton, in the name of the Father, and of the Son, and of the Holy Spirit." He placed his right hand on the back of Pete's head and his left hand on Pete's chest. He lowered him into the water.

And then it happened. Pete slipped. His feet went straight up to the top of the water. Everyone laughed as Bro. Jackie continually shouted at Pete to regain his footing. Bro. Jackie exclaimed, repeatedly, "Pete, get your feet! Pete, get your feet!"

Sunday school

Bro. Jackie was a strong believer in Sunday school. He used this tool effectively in growing the Pleasant Grove Baptist Church. He and I often spoke about "Flake's Formula." He had eagerly adopted and utilized this concept.

According to David Francis, Director of Sunday school for LifeWay in Nashville, Tennessee, "Arthur Flake [a layman] became the first leader of the Sunday School Department of the Baptist Sunday School Board in 1920."[32]

Flake's Formula for growing a Sunday school is composed of five steps:[33]

1. Know the possibilities
2. Enlarge the organization
3. Provide the space
4. Enlist and train the workers
5. Go after the people

Know the Possibilities

Before accepting the position as pastor of Pleasant Grove Bro. Jackie, a native-born "Moultonite," already knew where people lived, what they did for a living, and the types of people that would be most receptive to the Gospel. In short, he knew the possibilities.

---

[32] David Francis. The 5-Step Formula for Sunday school Growth (Nashville: LifeWay Press, 2005), 3.
    [33] Ibid., 3.

He had been a buyer in the cotton futures' market. He therefore knew, and understood, the farming community. He was well acquainted with the farmers in the area.

Bro. Jackie had also worked as a history teacher at the Speake School in Speake, Alabama. The school is located eight miles nearly due west of the Pleasant Grove Baptist Church. He had driven those eight miles daily, becoming familiar with "the lay of the land" that would eventually become the path of his first, and most successful, van route.[34]

As has been mentioned, Bro. Jackie had also been employed as an agent with the Horace Mann Educators Corporation. Through his work there he had, over the years, developed

---

[34] The Speake route not only reached the children in the area, but also their parents. We rerouted the van because all of the original van riders were now coming with their families.

many close relationships with the teachers and other school personnel in the Moulton area.

Enlarge the Organization

Bro. Jackie believed in starting new Sunday school classes. He instinctively knew that[35]:

> *New classes grow faster than established classes ... [and] new classes tend to visit more, reach more people, and witness to more people than established classes.*

Provide the Space

When Bro. Jackie arrived at Pleasant Grove, he discovered that the church had many empty classrooms. He quickly remedied that problem!

I can only go by observation at this point. But I believe that, when Bro. Jackie arrived at Pleasant Grove, he took the time to map out the

---

[35]

http://www.sschool.com/content/adultstart.htm, site visited on 3/13/2014.

facilities. He placed the nursery rooms closest to the sanctuary (since parents want easy access to their babies). The next sets of classrooms were assigned to the elderly members (due to mobility issues), then the children, the youth, and, finally, the young adults.

Under Bro. Jackie's leadership, Pleasant Grove Baptist Church was in a constant state of adding new buildings. According to an article in The Alabama Baptist newspaper:

> *Shelton also led Pleasant Grove Baptist through four major building programs — a family life center in 1987, a $1.3 million worship center in 1995, an office complex built in 1999 and a $1.85 million education building in 2002.*[36]

---

[36] "Moulton-area Church Marks 150 Years with Reflections of Past, Vision for Future." The Alabama Baptist. 7 December 2006.

Pleasant Grove Baptist Church

An aerial view of the church's facilities[37] is shown above (prior to the addition of the new education building in 2002). Buildings 1 through 5 are described below:

Building 1

The oldest sanctuary on the existing property. The building had already been converted to classroom space when Bro. Jackie arrived at the church in 1980.

---

[37] Picture taken from the cover of the <u>Pleasant Grove Baptist Church Directory</u> (Galion, OH: United Church Directories, circa 2003)

Building 2

The sanctuary Bro. Jackie inherited in 1980. The building has now been converted to an office complex and a large classroom.

Building 3

Originally constructed as a fellowship hall, this building housed an older adult men's Sunday school class.

Building 4

The Family Life Center, Bro. Jackie's first building project. The building was erected in 1987, just prior to my leaving Pleasant Grove to go to Ohio. The F.L.C. houses a commercial kitchen, a gymnasium, a couple of classrooms downstairs, several classrooms upstairs, and restrooms on both floors.

Building 5

The "new" auditorium. Bro. Jackie led the church to build this building toward the end of the 1980s. Construction was completed in 1995, three years after my return from Ohio.

The facility houses a 999-seat auditorium,[38] nursery space, and classrooms for senior adults.

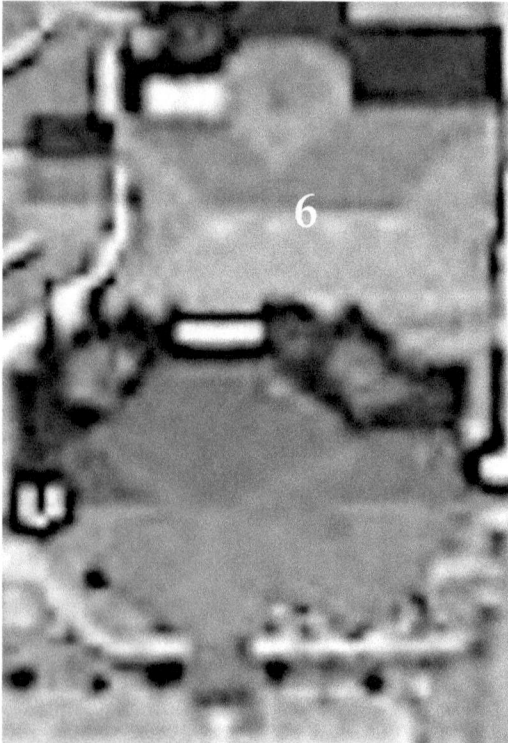

---

[38] At the time it was built, a 1,000 seat auditorium would have required the addition of a sprinkler system. Bro. Jackie opted to stay just below the requirement.

Building 6[39]

The new education building (see previous page). Although Bro. Jackie envisioned this building, he did not intend to construct it during his tenure at Pleasant Grove. The church leaders encouraged him to start the construction. Knowing that he could not start something that he did not intend to finish, he postponed his retirement until the building was completed and fully paid for in 2004. The building is named in his honor.

Enlist and Train the Workers

Bro. Jackie believed in training his workers. The local association sponsored an annual age-graded training conference for teachers and, you had better believe, we *all* attended!

---

[39] http://www.mapquest.com/#b15628d9b6fb3621bf015928, site visited on 2/20/2014.

In addition to the annual associational training conference, he also emphasized the Sunday evening Discipleship Training program.[40] He began building a "farm team" of teachers. As you can see from the somewhat sketchy graph below,[41] and the figures in Appendix B, attendance in Discipleship Training at Pleasant Grove would be considered phenomenal for a church of *any* size.

Discipleship Training
Average Attendance
1980 - 1993

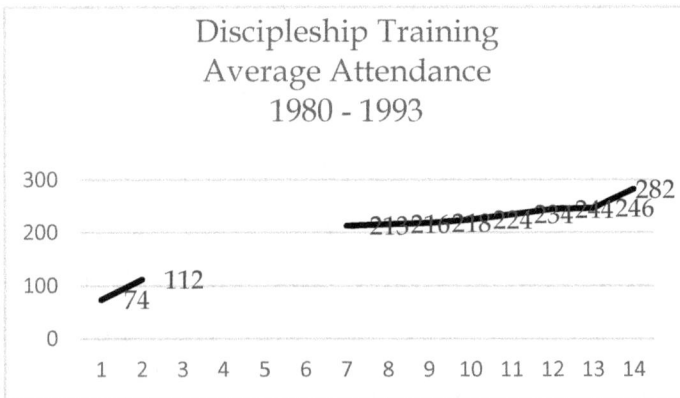

[40] [Training] opportunities to learn more about discipleship. Definition taken from http://going.imb.org/3yrsormore/details.asp?StoryID=7441&LanguageID=1709, site visited on 3/10/2014,

[41] Statistics for several years are unavailable. However, a pattern of sustained growth can be easily established.

Jackie Shelton

Bro. Jackie had a way of getting the church leaders involved. He *expected* people to do what he wanted.

One year, Pleasant Grove was hosting the Associational Music Festival, a medium for highlighting the choirs of the various churches. Bro. Jackie said something to the effect that, "I don't want us to be embarrassed tomorrow night. We are hosting this event, so we need to be on time. We need to have the most people of all of the churches. If we can't honor Jesus with our faithfulness, we won't participate in any of these events in the future."

For the record, we understood his message. We *were* on time, and we did *have* the largest group of people. And we did continue to participate in the ensuing years.

Enrollment

Bro. Jackie firmly believed in enrolling people in Sunday school. When he arrived at Pleasant Grove in 1980, many of the teachers had been seeking to improve their attendance *percentages*. In order to accomplish that objective, they were periodically removing the names of the less-than-faithful attendees from their class rolls. Bro. Jackie put an immediate stop to this practice.

Why? According to one source:[42]

> *When should people be removed from a class roll? Only in three instances: They move away, and it is obvious that they are not going to be back; they move their membership to another church, or begin attending another class in the same church; or, when they die.*

---

[42] http://www.trinityfulton.com/importance-of-sunday-school-enrollment, site visited on 2/21/2014.

Bro. Jackie took that advice one step further. In his mind, the only *two* ways to have your name removed from a class roll would be either through your death or through joining another church. He often reminded his teachers, "Many of the people that move away from the Moulton area will eventually return. By keeping them on our rolls, we will already have all of their personal information (birthdays, children's names, etc.), and we won't have to ask them for it again."

A popular topic at church growth conferences in the 1980s was known as the "Enrollment-Attendance Rule." The Rule stated, "On average, churches have a Sunday School *attendance* of 50% of their *enrollment*."[43] Ken Braddy concurred: "In almost any church,

---

[43] http://www.trinityfulton.com/site visited on 2/20/2014.

Sunday School attendance is approximately 50% of enrollment."[44]

So the obvious conclusion is the more people you enroll, the more people you will have in attendance. As stated in an article entitled, "The Importance of Sunday school Enrollment":[45]

> *Any class can have 100% attendance by simply taking non-attenders off their roll. It would be better to have 50% of 30 people than to have 100% of 10.*

Jackie revised the "Enrollment-Attendance Rule." We could refer to it as the "Jackie Shelton Rule." He made the decision to completely forget all of the percentages, and just keep on enrolling. In fact, the *lower* the

---

[44] http://texasbaptists.org/files/2012/10/Sunday-School-Enrollment.pdf, site visited on 2/20/2014.
[45] http://www.trinityfulton.com/site visited on 2/20/2014.

percentage, the *better* (See graph *below* and Appendix A)

Average Attendance vs. Percentage of Enrollment

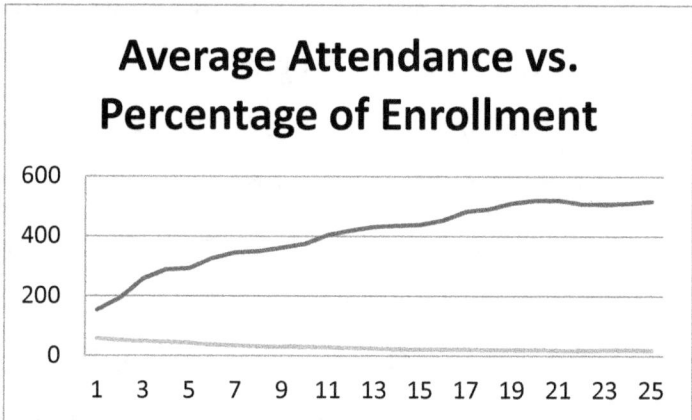

This is an extremely significant discovery. Without realizing it and, in spite of some of the criticisms he received from other pastors, Bro. Jackie had *revolutionized* the concept of Sunday school enrollment. The focus should not be on trying to approach 100%, as rural churches have been wont to do. Neither should the focus be on maintaining a 50% figure, as the "experts" have claimed that we should. Rather, we should strive to drive this percentage to the lowest point possible — in Bro. Jackie's case, 18% in 2001.

You might ask, "How did he do it? How did he enroll so many people?" He did it the old-fashioned way — by going to people's homes. He once told me that he had no use whatsoever for a computer. His words to me were, "You and Neil can have computers if you want, but I don't need one. The last time I checked, no computer has ever led anybody to personal faith in Jesus Christ."

And do you know what? He was right! He chose rather to utilize *his* time to literally go door-to-door for the purpose of meeting area residents. He would make several visits to the same homes, always looking for opportunities to share his Christian faith with anyone that he would meet.

He also kept a ready supply of enrollment forms with him, similar to the one pictured below:[46]

SUNDAY SCHOOL REGISTRATION

❏ *Enroll Me Today!*   Class Assigned: _____

❏ Thanks, but we're just visiting today.   Today's Date: _____

NAME			DATE OF BIRTH
SPOUSE'S NAME			DATE OF BIRTH
STREET ADDRESS		HOME PHONE	OFFICE PHONE
CITY		STATE	ZIP
EMAIL ADDRESS			

❏ I AM NOT A CHURCH MEMBER   ❏ I AM A MEMBER OF

CHILDREN'S NAMES	DATE OF BIRTH	SCHOOL GRADE	DEPARTMENT ASSIGNED

⊕ LifeWay

Whenever he discovered a person that was unaffiliated with a church, he would take out one of the cards. He would ask the person for their information and, voilà, they would be enrolled.

---

[46] Available through Lifeway Christian Resources in packs of 100 for $4.99 at the following web address: http://www.lifeway.com/Product/enrollment-card-permanent-record-of-progress-form-10-P001149148

I know what you are thinking. You are wondering, "Was it that simple?"

The answer is, "Yes," and "No."

Obtaining the information is simple. Making all of the visits is, however, very difficult. But Bro. Jackie was willing to sacrifice in order to make the visits.

On a Lighter Note

I once asked Bro. Jackie to share with me his secret for remembering people's names and their family relationships. I wanted to know his mnemonic device. I knew he had some sort of shortcut or trick. Frankly, I was quite envious of his ability.

He replied, "It's simple. When I end a home visit, I return to my car. I begin praying for the people *by name* that I have just met in that house. I keep praying until I remember their names, and then I crank the car and drive away."

I thought, "That's no secret! That's hard work!" And I was right. It was, and is, hard work. But so is staying motivated enough to make the visits. If you can make the visits and you can pray for the people until you remember their names, then you will have no problem filling out the enrollment cards.

The Myth of the Church Field

A church "field" is the area surrounding a particular church. I remember having seen a map of the locations of all of the local churches hanging on the wall of the break room of the Muscle Shoals Baptist Association. Someone had taken a compass, and had drawn a series of concentric circles around each church. The circles represented a five mile radius. A few of them overlapped, but only slightly.

Pleasant Grove Baptist Church's "center" is located in Wren, Alabama, at the intersection of Alabama State Highways 33 and 36. As you might have imagined, in Bro. Jackie's mind, the Pleasant Grove Church "field" encompassed many other churches' "fields."   In fact, Bro. Jackie habitually overstepped the boundaries of his church "field" as he visited people in an ever-growing area surrounding the church.

I believe Bro. Jackie's behavior stemmed, at least partially, from the fact that his father, Ernest Shelton, had been the circuit clerk[47] for thirty years. Having grown up in the home of a politician, Bro. Jackie knew the value of getting out and meeting the people throughout Lawrence County, Alabama.

You can see by the map[48] (on the next page) the area that he traveled, house by house.

---

[47] A county-wide position.

[48]

http://www.mapquest.com/#d841b86fd8999b2f868a156c, site visited on 2/20/2014.

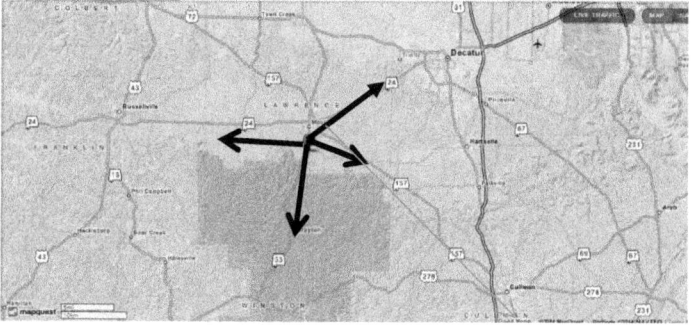

Follow-Up

As has been said, Bro. Jackie had very little use for a computer. He did, however, believe in the telephone. Every Monday morning, he would receive a printout of the Sunday school absentee list. He would make a personal call to every person that missed coming the day before!

He didn't stop there. On many occasions, while making his rounds to visit the unsaved and unchurched people of Lawrence County, Alabama, he would stop by to see the members of Pleasant Grove Baptist Church. He believed in the value of a personal touch—making contact with as many people as was humanly and, to be honest, superhumanly possible..

The Van Ministry

Bro. Jackie started the van ministry, a.k.a., the "bus" ministry prior to my joining the staff in 1984. His method for reaching children was simple:

- He would drive around the various neighborhoods on Saturday mornings, looking for signs of children playing.
- Upon finding the children, he would park his car and knock on the door.
- He would announce to the parents that we would have a church van available on Sunday mornings to pick up their children for church.
- CANDY—he would always have a generous supply of candy to give to the children![49]

---

[49] When I first started visiting my van routes, I didn't know about the candy. The kids would look disappointed when they realized that I was not Bro. Jackie. I later discovered his "secret" and bought a supply of candy of my own.

Jackie Shelton
His Best Sermon

Bro. Jackie's best sermon (in my most humble, but accurate, opinion) dealt with some opposition he was apparently receiving to the bus ministry. He preached the message during the summer of 1987.

The title of his message was, "We're Going Broke!" He preached it on a Sunday night. My wife, Diane, and I were sitting in the balcony, performing our usual "crowd control" duties.[50]

Bro. Jackie began his message using the tone of his detractors. It was almost like a song. The refrain was, "We're going Broke!" He said, "Folks, we're going broke. Ever since we started this bus ministry, it has done nothing but cost us a lot of money. First, we have to buy the vans, and they aren't cheap!"

---

[50] Keeping the children and young people from killing each other (just kidding).

"We're going broke!"

"But it doesn't stop there. We have to put gas in those vans. And you know how much gas costs nowadays."

"We're going broke!"

"And don't forget the tires. We will eventually have to put tires on these things. And the maintenance. What about the oil changes we will need just to keep them running?"

"We're going broke!"

"And they break down. We might have to replace a motor or a transmission. And you know how much those things cost."

"We're going broke!"

"And then they will eventually wear out. Can you believe it? We will actually have to replace some of these old ones with new ones. It's an endless cycle."

"We're going broke!"

"And don't forget the home lives of the children that ride our vans. They don't know how to act in church. And then these children will come into our fine facilities, take crayons, and mark all over the walls. So, one day, we will have to repaint the whole church."

"We're going broke!"

And then, right in the middle of the sermon, he stopped. He paused for effect. He swept the room with a penetrating stare. He looked into our souls. He made sure that he had everyone's attention (and he *did*). He became unusually serious. He resumed, "Listen, people. We are **not** going broke. When I came as your pastor in 1980, your offerings were only $60,000.00 a year. Last year, we collected more than $300,000.00!"

"And do you know why? Because God honors our willingness to reach out to these children that nobody else seems to want. And the minute we stop reaching out to them is the minute that He stops blessing us!"

"We can repaint the walls. We can replace the vans. But we cannot stop ministering to these children."

Wow! I was literally "blown away!" And guess what? The opposition immediately faded away. More vans and more routes would be added.

When my family and I returned to Pleasant Grove Baptist Church in 1992, I was placed in charge of the van ministry. I believe that we had four vans at the time—two Fords and two Dodges. Over time, we added two more vans, for a total of six.

Since I was also in charge of maintenance, I quickly observed the superiority of the Ford vans. As the equipment began to age, we replaced all of our Dodge vans with Fords.[51]

Our church name was placed on the sides of each of the vans. I then added numbers to the hoods—one through six.

Noticing the numbering system used on the local school buses, I changed our numbering system to reflect the model years of the vans. So we had 97-1, 98-1, etc.

On some years, we actually bought two vans. For instance, we had 99-1 and 99-2. After my departure, the church bought its first 2000 model year van. The number assigned was "00-1." One of the drivers said, jokingly, I want to drive van number 00-7![52]

---

[51] A couple of church members were loyal Dodge owners. They were not overly happy with my selection.
[52] A little "James Bond" humor.

Six Routes Going in Six Different Directions

I scheduled three or more drivers *per route* on six separate routes to pick up the children on Sunday mornings, Sunday nights, and Wednesday nights. Our drivers were literally "dropping like flies." I decided to stop pickups on Wednesday nights, limiting the drivers to Sunday services only.[53]

At that time, Pleasant Grove had three full-time staff members. Since the drivers were already overworked, we were each assigned two routes to visit *every* week. Bro. Jackie insisted that the three of us[54] would go out *every* Saturday morning to remind the children to get ready for the following Sunday morning.

---

[53] My successor, Jamin Grubbs, wisely revised the schedules for Sunday mornings and *Wednesday* nights. This aided in the growth of the youth ministry under his leadership.

[54] Bro. Jackie, Neil Carter, and I.

And he was right. On the Saturdays that any one of us had neglected to make our visits, our attendance numbers would suffer on the following Sundays. So there we would go, candy in hand, to talk to the kids *and* their parents. We made a point of always talking to the parents, because they would ultimately be responsible for ensuring that the kids would be ready when our vans arrived.

A Side Benefit

Through the van ministry, Bro. Jackie inadvertently stumbled upon the power of human curiosity. Curiosity may have "killed the cat," but it also "grew the church."

As human beings we are, by nature, curious creatures. We are inquisitive. The National Enquirer©, a supermarket tabloid, made an untold fortune with the slogan, "Enquiring minds want to know!"™

People, both in rural areas *and* in "the big

85

city" alike, are known for their inquisitive natures. Hence, we all have a shared compulsion known as "rubbernecking."

An abbreviated definition of the term is, "to look about, stare, or listen with exaggerated curiosity."[55] An expanded definition is:

> *The act of looking at something as you drive by. People do it when they come past an accident. Also tourists do it when they are observing the scenery when they are driving. It quite often causes traffic to slow down because the person looking generally slows down a bit to look out their window or windshield.*[56]

A Personal Illustration

For instance, when my wife, Diane, and I were dating, I had a wreck on the interstate in

---

[55] MERRIAM-WEBSTER'S COLLEGIATE DICTIONARY AND THESAURUS, DELUXE AUDIO EDITION®.

[56]

http://www.urbandictionary.com/define.php?term=rubber+necking, site visited on 2/28/2014.

downtown Atlanta, Georgia. When the police arrived, I asked them to contact my parents.

My dad, a salesman for Equitable Life, knew his way around town. He was familiar with all of the shortcuts and *longcuts* into the city. He often said, "I will drive the back roads to my office so that I can avoid the traffic."

My dad arrived about the same time as the ambulance. He checked on the condition of the injured man in the other car. He then turned his attention to me. He had the dreaded look.

He said, "Do you know why it took me so long to get here?" I shook my head. He continued, "Because the traffic is backed up for at least ten miles. Not only did *you* have a wreck, there is no telling how many wrecks that you have *caused*! People are all stopping to look at your car and, as a result, some of them are now having wrecks of their own."[57]

An Unforeseen Blessing

As you might have expected, we were attracting a lot of needy families through our van ministry at Pleasant Grove. Our benevolence budget was being stretched to its limit.

But, to my surprise, something else began to happen. Many professionals, such as doctors, teachers, and engineers, also began coming to the church.

At first this phenomenon seemed, to me, to be totally unrelated. Bro. Jackie explained it like this: "When people began to hear about the 'happenings' at Pleasant Grove—our large numbers of baptisms and all of the building projects—they had to come and see for

---

[57] My dad was not particularly known for being a man of great compassion.

themselves. And many of them have chosen to stay."

He concluded, "People *know* where God is at work, and they will *go* where He is at work. He is at work at Pleasant Grove."

Benevolence

Pleasant Grove had a thriving benevolence ministry. In addition to our coat closet, we also helped many needy families financially each year.

When I returned from Ohio, Bro. Jackie was typically giving out $100 per request per family. He also carried a stack of $20 bills that he could dispense whenever he saw a need (given to Bro. Jackie by various people for that expressed purpose).

All of the church staff members soon learned that, when a check or cash was given, the money would not always be used for its intended purpose. We developed a plan of distribution:

1. We kept a log book in the outer office to ensure that no family would receive assistance more than once in a 30-day period. They were required to wait until the next month.

2. We systematically reduced the amount of money we were giving to each family — from $100 to $50 to $25.

3. We developed a voucher system — a "check" — that could only be used at either the grocery store in town or the local gas station. Each month the businesses would send us the original copies of the vouchers, along with a bill for the total amount. We would, in turn, mail a check to them for the balance.

Dr. Reginald Barnard, professor of church history at Mid-America Baptist Theological Seminary, often said, "A large part of being in the ministry is having people take advantage of you." He further stated, "I would rather give assistance to several people that don't really need it than to risk not helping someone that does."

Noting his concerns, I have helped many people along the way. At Pleasant Grove, we have likely helped thousands.

One afternoon, a lady walked into my office. She explained to me that she and her children needed some food. I checked the log book. We had not helped this lady in the last 30 days.

Since, at that time, we had not reduced the amount we were typically giving, I filled out a voucher for her in the amount of $50.00. She thanked me and walked out of my office.

She returned moments later with another lady that she introduced as her sister. She said, "My sister needs some groceries, too."

I smiled as I said, "Okay. Just give the $50.00 voucher back to me."

As she extended her hand, I informed her, "I will give each of you a voucher for $25.00."

She withdrew her hand. She clutched the $50.00 voucher tightly with both hands. She turned away as she said, "My sister doesn't need any help."

And then she, sister in tow, quickly departed.

His Techniques

According to Webster, one definition of the word "technique" is, "A method of accomplishing a desired aim." Bro. Jackie had an assortment of techniques, or methods, that he frequently used in growing Pleasant Grove Baptist Church.

Influence the Influencers

Rural churches are bastions of political power. As a rural pastor, you can either fight the system, or you can embrace the system and use it to your advantage.

Bro. Jackie, as has been mentioned, grew up in the home of the circuit clerk of Lawrence County, Alabama. Bro. Jackie understood the small town politics of the local church.

Accordingly, he had discovered the secret of influencing the influencers long before he had arrived at Pleasant Grove. He knew that, before he could ever bring a major directive before the church, he would need to garner the votes of both the formal and informal leaders in the church. He would, essentially, need to influence the influencers.

Many times, especially in rural churches, the power will be closely held within a select group known as either the *deacons* or the *elders*. Many an unsuspecting pastor has walked into his new church, thinking that *he* is now in charge. That, my friends, will be a *big* mistake.

Countless jokes have been told about the conflict between pastors and deacons. The pastor may believe that he has the *scriptural* right to lead but, in many cases, he does not have the *traditional* right to lead.

I personally believe there are two main reasons for why many, if not most, rural churches are lay-led rather than pastor-led. First, the pastor (with the exception of a few men like Jackie Shelton) is, in all likelihood, "not from around here."

If you are new to the rural church scene, you might be asking, "What difference does that make?" Jason Huffman, associate pastor and youth director at the First United Methodist Church of Palestine, Texas, stated[58]:

> *In small towns, people can be funny about outsiders. There's no written policy about how new people are to be treated. However, it will take several years before you feel like you are a part of the fabric of the community. This includes church relationships, but also relationships in the community as well. Particularly if it is a small town of people who have been there a long time and are all connected to the same primary industry, it will be difficult to feel like you are a part of the "in crowd" until you've been there a while.*

Second, the lay leadership structure has evolved in the church *by necessity.* It was expedient.

I have frequently heard the term "not from around here" as I have served for more than two decades in rural churches in north

---

[58]

http://jasonbhuffman.wordpress.com/2011/02/14/things-to-know-about-rural-church-ministry/, site visited on 2/21/2014.

Alabama. I once said in a sermon, "Jesus came from Heaven. I guess *He* was not from around here, either!"

Obviously, it must not be a good thing if you are "not from around here." So, what does that term mean? It is akin to the popular statement, "Bless his heart." According to the Urban Dictionary™:

> *[Bless your heart] is a term used by the people of the southern United States particularly near the Gulf of Mexico to express to someone that they are an idiot without saying such harsh words.*[59]

It also means, "You are an idiot, but I like you and care about you, so I don't want to hurt your feelings."[60]

Financial expert Dave Ramsey concurred. He tweeted, "'With all due respect,' 'No offense.'

---

[59] http://www.urbandictionary.com/define.php?term=bless+your+heart, site visited on 3/2/2014.

[60] Ibid.

'Bless your heart,' and 'Just sayin'…are all lies at the end of an insult."[61]

When rural church folks say that their pastor is "not from around here," they are mockingly explaining to each other why he doesn't understand the way things work in their church. He doesn't have a grasp on how things have always *been* done, and will always *be* done. In a nutshell, he doesn't understand their traditions.

Rural pastor, fight it if you will. Be sure and point out to your folks that the Pharisees were also the masters of tradition. Don't forget to remind the people, "If you always do what you've always done, you'll always get what you

---

61

https://twitter.com/DaveRamsey/status/4401365943437 39394, site visited on 3/2/2014.

always got, and you'll always feel what you always felt."[62]

Go ahead and make your changes. Flex your spiritual muscles. However, you will soon discover the truth of the statement that I heard frequently at the seminary, "If you make too many changes too quickly, the only thing that will change is the [pastor's] name on the church sign."

Second, not only are you "not from around here," the lay leaders are simply responding to the fact that they have been "caught holding the bag" many times in the past.

Several years ago, some new pastor came in with his newfangled ideas. The church members supported him, invested a lot of their

---

[62]
http://www.searchquotes.com/quotation/If_you_always _do_what_you%27ve_always_done%2C_you%27ll_alway s_get_what_you_always_got%2C_and_you%27ll_always_ f/288393/, site visited on 3/2/2014.

money and other resources, and implemented his plans. And then he left. The next pastor repeated the process. And then he left.

Eventually some deacon, or group of deacons, stepped in to "straighten up the mess." And so year after year, pastor after pastor, the deacons (or elders) have picked up where the departing pastors have left off.

They have made the unspoken decision, "We will never allow this to happen to us again!" They have thereby assumed the task of leading the church—regardless of whether the church is currently with or without a pastor.

Again, rural pastor, fight it if you will. But the wise pastor has both learned and applied the truth of an oft-quoted statement by motivational speaker and former pastor John C. Maxwell, "He that thinketh he leadeth, and hath no one following him, is only taking a walk." Bro. Jackie was a wise rural pastor.

Bro. Jackie clearly understood the power structure in the typical rural church. Having personally served as a deacon at Moulton Baptist Church, he had learned how to work within the framework of a deacon body. He was able to successfully navigate the perilous waters of proposing major initiatives in the church.

His First Test

Steep Hollow had quickly outgrown their facilities. Bro. Jackie knew that the church needed to add educational space. What should he do about it? He did *not* bring up his observation from the pulpit, at least not initially. Rather, he approached a few of the "movers and shakers," the lay leaders and major financial contributors, in the church to present his idea. He solicited their input. He allowed them to "place their brands" on his plans. And then he gave them the credit for the proposal.

Having receiving the endorsement of the leaders, he began to inform the members of the church. The members, in turn, privately asked the lay leaders, the people they had learned to trust over the years, "What do *you* think we should do?" These leaders, already on board with the idea, said, "We think it's time to do this. We need more space. Let's do it."

The matter was closed. The buildings were built. And everyone was happy.

Bro. Jackie left Steep Hollow, but he did not forget this important lesson. He quickly determined that Pleasant Grove Baptist Church's leadership structure resided with the deacons. He would use that knowledge to his advantage, and to the advantage of the church.

I soon discovered his secret. On any given Sunday, someone would make a decision for Christ. Bro. Jackie would ask the question, "How do you feel about this decision?"

Our chairman of deacons would routinely reply, "I move that they be received."

Bro. Jackie would continue, "And all the people said…"

And then the church members, in unison, would say, "Amen."

Former president Harry S. Truman was correct when he said, "It is amazing what you can accomplish if you do not care who gets the credit."[63]

On a Lighter Note

Disclaimer: There is absolutely no comparison between the characters in the following story and the leadership at Pleasant Grove Baptist Church. Also, there is absolutely no similarity between Pleasant Grove's chairman of deacons and John Maxwell's "Gus." I am simply sharing the following story as an illustration of the

---

[63]

http://www.brainyquote.com/quotes/quotes/h/harrystr u109615.html, site visited on 3/2/2014.

power of the principle of influencing the influencers.

Motivational speaker John C. Maxwell related the following story several years ago at a conference that some friends and I attended at the Church at Brook Hills in Birmingham, Alabama: "My first church was located in a rural farming community in Indiana. I had been preaching there for a few weeks when one of the men, 'Gus,' asked me if I would like to attend the church's board meeting. I said that I would."

"The night of the meeting came. Gus called the meeting to order. And then he made his first motion. A man named Sid seconded the motion. And everyone around the table said, 'Amen.'"

"It went just like that all night long. And then Gus asked me, 'Pastor, would you like to close in prayer?' I said, 'Yes, Bro. Gus, I surely would.'"

W. Scott Moore

"Seeing how things were done in the church, I made a decision. I said to myself, 'If I am going to get anything done in this church, I will need to influence this influencer.'"

"I approached Gus before the next board meeting. I said, 'you know, Bro. Gus, I grew up on a farm (Bro. Gus, coincidentally, owned a farm). I would really appreciate it if you would let me come out some morning to help you with the chores.'"

"Gus jumped at the chance of having some free help. He said, 'Sure, pastor—if you think you can keep up.' I assured him that I could."

"And so, the following Saturday morning, I drove to Gus' farm. He and I repaired fences, fed the animals, and tore down an old barn. We worked hard!"

"When we finished, he and I sat on a couple of old tree stumps. We wiped the sweat

104

off of our foreheads. Gus looked at me and said, 'Pastor, I'm impressed. You really do know how to work!'"

"I thanked him. And then he asked the million-dollar question: 'Pastor, is there anything on your mind? Is there anything that you think we should do at the church?'"

"I replied, 'Well, Bro. Gus, since you have asked, there is one thing…'"

"What's that, pastor?"

"Bro. Gus, have you noticed that the paint is peeling off of the front door of the church?"

"Gus replied, 'No, pastor, I hadn't noticed.'"

"I continued, 'Well, Bro. Gus, it is. In fact, it looks like an alligator's hide. And the problem is that the front door is someone's first impression of our church. I think we should repaint it.'"

"He smiled and said, 'Done.   Is there anything else?'"

"'Yes, Bro. Gus,' I said. 'Have you been down in the basement lately?'"

"No, pastor, I haven't."

"Bro. Gus, the basement is full of water. There are tadpoles swimming around down there."

"I will take care of it, pastor.   Anything else?"

"Yes, Bro. Gus, there is one more thing. Our church is growing. We need more space. All of our existing classrooms are filled."

"Gus interrupted, 'That's true pastor. What can we do about it?'"

"I replied, 'There is a room, just outside of my office, that is piled full of junk. We could clean it out and make it into a classroom.'"

"Gus smiled as we finished our time together. A week or so passed. And then we held our next board meeting."

"As usual, Gus called the meeting to order. After small talk, he said, 'has anyone noticed our front door?'"

"'What about it?' Sid asked."

"Gus continued, 'The paint is peeling off of it. It looks like an alligator's hide. And that is someone's first impression of our church. I make a motion that we paint it.'"

"Sid chimed in, 'I second the motion.' The people said, 'Amen.' And the date was set for the project."

"Gus continued, 'Has anyone been down in the basement lately?'"

"The others exchanged nervous glances."

"Gus said, 'It's full of water. And there are tadpoles swimming around down there. I will be here on Saturday to work on it. Who will join me?' Several hands were raised."

"I have one more item. Our church is growing. We have completely run out of classroom space. I make a motion that we clean out the office just outside of the pastor's study so we can use it for a new classroom."

"Sid seconded the motion. The people said, 'Amen.' And the matter was settled."

"Gus then looked at one of the ladies. He said, 'And Sue, when we start the new class, I want you to teach it.'"

"Sue began to cry. She wiped away the tears. She said, 'I don't know if I am qualified to be a good teacher. But, Bro. Gus, if you and Jesus want me to teach it, I will give it my best.'"

Maxwell went on to say that Gus had become a powerful ally. When Maxwell's plan to build some additional space had been rejected by the District Superintendent, Gus simply said, "I will handle it."

Gus made one phone call to the Superintendent. He explained to the man the reasons why they wanted to build.

The Superintendent contacted Maxwell. He said, "You go ahead with your building."

Maxwell's Warning

John C. Maxwell concluded his story with this word of warning: "I heard that the church in Indiana had called a new pastor. I made arrangements to take him out to lunch. I explained the process to him that I have just explained to you."

"He didn't receive it well. He said, 'That may have worked for you, but I don't believe in playing games. I am the new pastor. I am the leader. And the church will do things my way.'"

"I smiled as I paid the bill. I said, 'I will be praying for you.' He thanked me, and we parted ways." A year later, not-so-mysteriously, the new pastor resigned.

An Amendment to the Story

Brother Jackie didn't always believe in "leading from behind." A clue to this fact was conspicuously placed on his desk.

After working on his sermons, he would place his pen and highlighter in the drawer. He would then tuck the sermon neatly inside his Bible, and place the Bible precisely on his desk.

He had the usual family pictures that faced him as he did his daily work. He also had some stacked in-and-out files on the left side of his desk.

The only thing that didn't seem to belong on his desk was a small, framed quotation. When I asked about it, he informed me that Ben-Ann had cross-stitched it for him.

The reason this item didn't seem to belong was that it faced *away* from Bro. Jackie.

110

In other words, it wasn't placed there for *his* benefit—it was placed there for the benefit of others. In other words, he wanted to make sure that people understood the message. Though humorous, the message clearly explained Bro. Jackie's philosophy of leadership to anyone that had dared to venture into his office: "If Moses had been a committee, the Israelites would still be in Egypt!"

De-Emphasize Preaching

In 2005, I invited Bro. Jackie to speak to the pastors of the Franklin Baptist Association in Russellville, Alabama. At the time, he had been retired from Pleasant Grove Baptist Church for a little over a year.

He now felt that he could safely share his heart with us. He said, "When I arrived at Pleasant Grove Baptist Church in 1980, I had a decision to make. I could either spend my time researching and writing sermons, or I could use it making a lot of visits every day."

He further stated, "I chose to make the visits. I had a backlog of sermons from my years back at Steep Hollow. I preached those old messages instead of developing a lot of new ones."

He concluded, "I know some of you think that I should have spent more time in sermon preparation, and maybe I should. But I stick by my choice. I believe it was the right one." Knowing the history of Pleasant Grove Baptist Church, nobody in the room dared to question his decision.

On a Lighter Note

You may be like the pastor that felt really encouraged about his message on one particular Sunday. He asked his wife, "Honey, how many really great preachers do you think there are in the world today."

Grinning, she replied, "One less than you think!"

On Another Lighter Note

Several of our senior adults traveled from Pleasant Grove to the Bellevue Baptist Church in Cordova, Tennessee. Our chairman of deacons[64] returned with the following report:

"That is an amazing church! The buildings are huge! We met a fellow whose full-time job is to change light bulbs. That's right. His job is to walk around the various buildings, locate the bulbs that have burned out, and replace them."

The chairman of deacons continued, showing his respect and admiration for Bro. Jackie, "And, I must admit, that Adrian Rogers is a very good preacher. But he doesn't hold a

---

[64] He was also the teacher of the Sunday school class that Diane and I attended.

113

candle to our pastor. Bro. Jackie can outpreach him any day!"

Emphasize Evangelism

Bro. Jackie was very sensitive, and somewhat defensive, about the fact that he had chosen to focus on winning souls rather than on discipling people. His remarks at the Franklin Association Pastors' Conference revealed to those of us that were present the fact that he had been criticized many times for his lack of personal involvement in helping his new converts grow to spiritual maturity.

His response to us was, "The last time I checked, if someone accepts Jesus Christ as his or her Lord and Savior, regardless of whether or not they grow spiritually, they will go to Heaven. I may not have been the best at follow-up, but I have led many people to Christ. And I am satisfied with my decision."

114

Know the Audience

Bro. Jackie was well aware of the fact that the primary group of people that he would be required to please would be those who had been born before 1946, alternately known as the "Builder Generation," the "Matures," or the "Silent Generation."

Members of the "Builder Generation" have many fine qualities. They:[65]

- Respond well to teaching
- Sacrifice [themselves] for others
- Focus on group goals
- Share common values, ethics (honesty, morality)
- Pull together (they won WWII)
- Are loyal to the institution
- Base their success on family and their community

---

[65] http://50alive.com/gpage2.html, site visited on 2/25/2014.

115

- Believe in leadership by command; they follow directions
- Ask, "What can I do for God?"
- Also ask, "How can I help the church?"

Negatively, they "are resistant to change."[66]

An article entitled, "Employee and Organizational Development,"[67] published by the Texas A&M University in College Station, Texas, listed twelve suggestions for working with members of this age group. Note by the *italicized* additions to the statements below that Bro. Jackie instinctively followed many of these suggestions:

1. Emphasize their loyalty

---

[66] http://50alive.com/gpage2.html, site visited on 2/25/2014.

[67] http://eodinfo.tamu.edu/media/80952/generations.pdf, site visited on 2/25/2014/

2. Be open and honest — *Bro. Jackie believed in transparency regarding the finances* (see "Increase the Giving" below)

3. Acknowledge, value, and seek insights from their experience, expertise, and dedication — *Bro. Jackie consistently sought counsel from our deacon chairman* (see "Lead through Others" below)

4. Provide traditional incentives such as plaques

5. Make changes slowly; don't surprise them — *Bro. Jackie would take great pains to ensure that the people were "on board" before starting major building projects*

6. Make announcements well in advance — *Bro. Jackie personally read the announcements to the church members before the worship services*

7. Notify them of your experience and credentials — *Bro. Jackie frequently*

reminded us of his spiritual discipline, his educational attainments, and his business acumen

8. Be a degree more formally dressed than your team (if the majority comes from this generation) — *Bro. Jackie always dressed professionally* (see "His Image")

9. Speak more formally and profession- ally

10. Communicate with handwritten memos, letters, and personal notes

11. Use surnames and titles; ask their permission before you address them by their first name — *Bro. Jackie addressed all of the older men as "Brother."*

12. Provide clear lines of command

Be On-Time

To Bro. Jackie, being on-time was a nonnegotiable item. I was destined to learn that lesson on my first day at Pleasant Grove in 1984.

The "Ground Rules"

My family and I had packed all of our belongings into the U-Haul™ truck that the church had rented for us. Bro. Jackie had enlisted helpers in shifts to help us unload: "If they get here between 2:00 and 4:00 in the afternoon, you folks can help. Between 4:00 and 6:00, you other folks can help."

Due to our lack of helpers on the Memphis side, however, we didn't arrive at the old parsonage in Moulton until 11:00 that night. But nobody complained. The men busied themselves, unloading the truck, assembling the beds, and arranging the furniture. One man even offered to return the truck to the rental location for us the next morning.

Diane and I placed our three tired children in their beds. At 3:00 a.m. on Sunday, we were finally settling down to sleep. Diane heard a noise. She asked, "What was that?"

I heard an unfamiliar sound. "Moo." I said, "I *think* it's a cow."

Having grown up in the city of Atlanta, Georgia, Diane said, "We're here, aren't we?"

I said, "Yes, dear. We are here."

Sunday school at Pleasant Grove Baptist Church started promptly at 9:30 a.m. or, sometimes, sooner (remember — Bro. Jackie was always early and never late) with what they called an "Opening Assembly" — basically, a meeting of all of the adult class members and teachers for a brief meeting and a devotional. I strolled in at 9:35. I was proud that I was only five minutes late.

A bell began to ring, signifying the time to end the Opening Assembly and to go to the regular classes. Bro. Jackie met me at the door. I could tell by the look on his face that something was troubling him. He said, "I need to meet with you in my office." He led the way down the dark and narrow corridor. I timidly followed.

He said, "Close the door." When I did, he pointed to a vinyl covered, heavily padded, brown pew that ran the length of the right wall of his office. He asked me to sit down.

I'm not sure, but I think a trail of sweat began to run down the side of my face. With a serious look and unfriendly, narrowed eyes, he said:

> *I have worked hard for these last four years to make sure that we start on time. When I got here, people just showed up and started their services whenever they got ready. I now have things starting on time. I know you didn't get to bed until late last night, so I am going to let it go this time. But it had better not happen again. Do we understand each other?*

121

I said, "Yes, sir." He then instructed me to go to my class. As you might imagine, I was never late again. In fact, I usually arrived 20 to 30 minutes early to all of the activities at the church! Come to think of it, 15 years after the last time I worked with Bro. Jackie, I *still* make a point of being early for every meeting!

Why?

Why was Bro. Jackie so interested in starting everything on time? I am sure there are many reasons. Having been a school teacher and a businessman, punctuality had been an essential part of his professions.

But, I believe, it was more than that. I believe it was also an effort on his part to meet the needs of those people that made up the leadership core of the church. They were the most likely to be concerned as to whether or not the services started on time.

Jackie Shelton

You ask, "Which group was that?" It was, unquestionably, the "Builder Generation."[68]

On a Lighter Note

One of the Brotherhood[69] Directors from yesteryear at Pleasant Grove was working feverishly to help his cooks prepare the morning's meal for the men that would soon begin to arrive. As was his custom, Bro. Jackie asked the Director if we could start eating a few minutes early.

The Brotherhood Director called on one of the men to pray, and then immediately started serving the breakfast. He leaned over to me. He whispered, in a lighthearted jest, "We'd better go ahead and get started. We wouldn't want to be *artificially late*."

---

[68] See "Know the Audience" above.

[69] "Brotherhood" at Pleasant Grove was a monthly gathering of men on a Sunday morning for a meal, a time of fellowship, and a message from a guest speaker.

123

The K.I.S.S. Formula

The K.I.S.S. Formula has been around for a long time. It stands for, "Keep it simple, stupid!" Bro. Jackie "kept things simple" at Pleasant Grove. He repeatedly stressed two, and *only* two, spiritual disciplines—attendance and giving. As a result, everybody knew what was important to Bro. Jackie.

Vacations

Bro. Jackie, as has been mentioned, frequently vacationed at Bluewater Bay in Niceville, Florida. When he would return to the church, he would bring back bulletins from the church he had visited. He expected all of his church members, and especially his staff members, to do the same.

I remember "backsliding" only one time. The Spanish mackerel were running in the waters of the gulf off of the end of the state pier in Gulf Shores, Alabama. I simply could not leave.

I must confess that I have never told Bro. Jackie about the incident. He *may*, however, have something to say about my infraction when I see him again in Heaven!

Hire Some Help

Although Bro. Jackie did not attend the Mid-America Baptist Theological Seminary, he fully supported its strong stances regarding the Bible and personal evangelism. He not only endorsed the *mission* of Mid-America mission, he also made a sizable financial investment in the seminary throughout the years.

For those reasons, when he needed to hire his first full-time staff member in 1984, he made a trip to Memphis, Tennessee. He spoke with the seminary president, Dr. Gray Allison. He told Dr. Gray, "I am looking for a man that knows how to work hard and win souls."

Dr. Gray replied, "Scott Moore."

Bro. Jackie also contacted his former pastor, Dr. Phil Allison. Again he asked, "I need somebody that knows how to work hard and can win souls." Unaware of his brother's response, Dr. Phil said, "Scott Moore."

I had completed my four-year stint at the seminary just a few months earlier. Although I was a recent graduate, I was still pumping gas at Bob McVay, Sr.'s Amoco. The gas station was located at the corner of Union Avenue and North Cooper Street in rugged midtown Memphis, Tennessee. I often joked with my fellow "pump-jockeys" that I was planning to hang my Master's degree over one of the gasoline pumps. I was also going to inform the customers that their gas had been installed by an attendant with a Master's degree.

I was, as you might imagine, a little frustrated! I felt like one of the workers in Jesus' parable:[70]

> *And about the eleventh hour he went out, and found others standing idle, and saith unto them, "Why stand ye here all the day idle?" They say unto him, "Because no man hath hired us." He saith unto them, "Go ye also into the vineyard; and whatsoever is right, that shall ye receive."*

I eventually received two phone calls that would radically change my life. The first call was from the seminary, informing me that a pastor from Alabama would be contacting me about a possible job—as a *youth* minister! I almost laughed. I thought to myself, "What do I know about working with teenagers?"

For one thing, I had never worked with young people. My primary ministry had been with children at the Bellevue Baptist Church.

---

[70] Matthew 20:6-7.

Second, I had been called to preach. How could this possibly be a fulfillment of that calling?

The second phone call I received was from Jackie Ray Shelton. Bro. Jackie was the pastor of the Pleasant Grove Baptist Church in Moulton, Alabama. My name had come up twice in his discussions with both Dr. Phil and Dr. Gray Allison. Jackie had apparently asked for a graduate that knew how to work (I had two jobs while simultaneously attending classes at the seminary) and was a soul-winner (I made regular visits to the local housing project to share my faith).

We scheduled a time to meet at the gas station when he and his wife would be on their return trip to Alabama. A few minutes before our scheduled time,[71] a very clean, white, late-model Buick pulled onto the lot. The car slowed to a stop at the full-service pumps — a somewhat

---

[71] Bro. Jackie was *always* early; he was *never* late.

unusual occurrence. A well-dressed, white-haired man opened the driver's side door and stepped out of the vehicle. He approached one of my fellow workers with the question, "Is Scott Moore here?" My buddy pointed in my direction.

"There's a guy here to see you," the other pump-jockey said. I sprinted over to the car. "Brother Jackie?" I asked.

"Yes," he replied. "You must be Scott." I nodded.

He introduced me to his wife, Ben-Ann. As I recall, she remained in the car while I filled their tank and conversed with her husband.

Bro. Jackie began to share his vision of reaching Moulton, Alabama, with me. "I want to build the greatest rural church in America." He continued, "And I need a youth minister to help me do it. I would like for you to pray about it. You can call me and let me know what you decide."

He handed his business card to me. And then he and Ben-Ann drove off into the sunset. Actually, they were heading east—but you get the picture...

I couldn't wait to tell the good news to my wife, Diane. "A pastor came to the gas station today. I think that he wants to offer me a job!"

Needless to say, Diane was thrilled. As a school teacher, she had carried the financial load for our family of five for the previous four years. Now it would become my turn.

I called Bro. Jackie to tell him that we were interested. He scheduled a date for our family to come to Pleasant Grove Baptist Church. The purpose of our visit would be to allow the church members to have the opportunity to meet us and to ask questions.

"Oh, and by the way," he said, "you will be preaching on Sunday."

Having preached only a handful of times, I informed him that I was a little unprepared. He said, "Don't worry. I will let them know that we are considering calling you to be our *youth* pastor, not *the* pastor."

Our First Visit to Moulton

The five of us piled into our blue 1978 Chevrolet Monte Carlo. We drove the 200 plus miles in approximately three-and-one-half hours on a Saturday morning. Bro. Jackie and Ben-Ann graciously allowed us to stay in the guest bedroom of their large, ranch-style parsonage located, providentially, less than a mile from the Deer Run Golf Course.

Bro. Jackie and Ben-Ann were a great host and hostess. Bro. Jackie made a point of conversing with our children. Our oldest child, Michael, really impressed him. Bro. Jackie noticed that he had a small, leathery E. T. action figure.[72] Jokingly, Bro. Jackie said to Michael, "I like your little doll."

Michael looked Bro. Jackie right in the eye. He countered, "It's not a doll. It's a stuffed animal."

Bro. Jackie looked at me. He said, "You'd better watch out for that one — he's smart!"[73]

The next morning, I preached at Pleasant Grove Baptist Church. As promised, Bro. Jackie told the congregation that I was not "trying out" for the job of pastor. If the church members made the decision to call me, I would become their *youth* minister and *associate* pastor. I was extremely thankful for his disclaimer!

---

[72] Extra-terrestrial, taken from the Steven Spielberg movie, "E. T."

[73] Parenthetically, Bro. Jackie was right. Michael, now known as "Mike," has a degree in Aeronautical Engineering. He is now working as the proverbial "rocket scientist."

After the service, Bro. Jackie and I stood on opposite sides of the back doorway so that we could shake hands with the departing congregants. One of the men chose to go out through Bro. Jackie's side. He shook hands with Bro. Jackie. He said, "That was a great sermon, pastor."

Bro. Jackie later told me, "I *thought* that guy was never listening to my sermons. Now I *know* it!"

After the service, we enjoyed a Southern favorite — a potluck dinner. For those of you in the other parts of the country, a "potluck" is a meal consisting of favorite dishes prepared by the church members and proudly displayed on long serving tables. The members then file along both sides of the tables, sampling a little of this and a lot of that. They are fabulous!

Diane, Michael, Kelly (our oldest daughter), and Susanna (still an infant), and I enjoyed our meals. Afterwards, some of the ladies offered to take care of Susanna, while "The Inquisition" was launched.

I don't remember any of the questions that I was asked. Neither do I remember all of the questioners. I do, however, remember one person in particular—one of the deacons, Jerry Armor. *Doctor* Jerry Armor. He asked me several thought-provoking questions. Fortunately, I was able to answer them to his satisfaction. He looked with an approving smile at Bro. Jackie. His smile was the equivalent of a "thumbs up."

The five of us piled back into the Monte Carlo. Bro. Jackie reached through the open window of the car to shake my hand. He then gave an envelope to me. "What's this?" I asked.

He replied, "That is for your mileage to and from the church. Be careful going home."

I thanked him, placed the car in gear, and drove off. I handed the envelope to Diane. She opened it. When she told me the amount of the enclosed check, we couldn't believe it — $150.00! Needless to say, Diane and I were extremely impressed with the generosity of Bro. Jackie and the people of Pleasant Grove Baptist Church!

Preparation

While waiting for the results of the upcoming business meeting at Pleasant Grove that would decide my fate, I spoke with a friend and fellow seminarian named Don Minshew. He recommended that I obtain and read a book written by Lawrence O. Richards, simply entitled, Youth Ministry.[74]

I followed Don's advice. I bought the book and studied it. I mapped out my strategy for youth ministry using the "What — so what"

---

[74] Lawrence O. Richards. Youth Ministry (Grand Rapids: Zondervan Publishing Corp., 1972).

135

technique. I would ask the kids, "*What* does the Bible say?" And then I would ask, "So what?" What difference does it make? What should be the application for our daily lives?[75]

The Phone Call

A few days later, our telephone rang. Bro. Jackie informed me that the consensus of the committee members was to call me to be their associate pastor. He wisely said, "I *could* call a special meeting for the purpose of voting on this recommendation. But I have decided that we are going to wait until the next regularly scheduled business meeting. This is an extremely important decision. I don't want anybody to be able to come back later — and they would — and say, 'I didn't know anything about the recommendation.' This way, everyone will

---

[75] Some of the teenagers would later confess, "When you taught the Bible, we thought 'So what!'"

be informed and will have the opportunity to vote."

Two weeks later, I received another phone call. Bro. Jackie told me the church members had voted to call me to the position. He also told me the percentage, but I don't remember the exact figure. He said, "You had a few negative votes, but don't take it personally. The people weren't voting against *you* — they were against calling you because *I* had recommended it!"

On a Lighter Note

I have learned over the years to be relatively unconcerned about the percentage of a vote. When my family and I returned from Ohio to work with Bro. Jackie in 1992, he said, excitedly, "You got a 100% vote!"

I said, "Do you know what that tells me?"

Bro. Jackie replied, "What?"

I said, "*Somebody* didn't vote!"

And then we shared a laugh. Instinctively, we both knew that what I had said had been true.

His Guidance

Having discovered "the ground rules" on my first Sunday at Pleasant Grove (see page 119), I met *promptly* with Bro. Jackie at 8:00 the next morning. This would be our first staff meeting. He seemed to have "gotten over" the fact that I had been late to the Opening Assembly. In fact, he never mentioned it again.

Instead, he shared with me, "You are the first full-time staff member, other than the pastor, that this church has ever called. I know that you have been called to preach, and that this probably won't be the last stop for you. So I am counting on you to do a good job, and to really work hard. If the church has a good experience with you, it will be that much easier for me to hire the next staff member."

138

I nodded in agreement.

He paused in order to change directions. Resuming, he said, "As far as what I want you to do, I did *not* hire you to help me do my job. I plan to keep doing everything that I am already doing. The reason I have brought you on board is so that you can find your own ministry here. I don't expect you to hit the ground running. I know that it will take a while for you to find your niche."

He continued, "And don't get tempted to do busy work—finding something to do when you really don't have anything that you need to do. The 'nature of the beast' of the ministry is that there will be times when you have nothing to do. Enjoy those times. There will be plenty of times when you will be so busy that you won't be able to catch your breath. Just do what you need to do, and I will be satisfied."

I was astonished. Was this the same man that I had met with just one day previously? The answer was, "Yes."

On a Lighter Note

My family and I had recently returned from leading a youth mission trip to Ohio. We had been making plans to leave Pleasant Grove and to move to Ohio so that I could work as the pastor of a mission church. Unaware of this development, one of the deacons suggested that the church purchase a new car for me.[76]

In light of my circumstances I could not, in good conscience, accept such a gift. Bro. Jackie came to the rescue! He offered to give me his 1969 gold Volkswagen Beetle that he had driven since his days in rural Mississippi. It was

---

[76] The deacons at Pleasant Grove Baptist Church had just voted to buy a new car for Bro. Jackie, something they did periodically because of the enormous amount of miles he placed on his cars.

in mint condition, with a little less than 500,000 miles on the original engine.

The longevity of Bro. Jackie's Volkswagen was legendary. It reminded all of us of the Israelites' experience in the wilderness. Moses reminded them, "Thy raiment waxed not old upon thee, neither did thy foot swell, these forty years."[77] He reiterated, "And I have led you forty years in the wilderness: your clothes are not waxen old upon you, and thy shoe is not waxen old upon thy foot."[78]

I gratefully accepted his gift. Since I fancied myself as somewhat of a mechanic, I bought the Chilton© repair manual for that particular model year of Volkswagen. I followed the instructions (or so I thought), and adjusted the valves. Within a couple of weeks, the engine locked up.

---

[77] Deuteronomy 8:4.
[78] Deuteronomy 29:5.

Bro. Jackie reminded the deacons that, since they had been willing to buy a new car for me, the church should be willing to pay for a new engine for the Volkswagen. They agreed, and the motor was replaced.

I had also bought new radial tires for the car, and it was ready to go! Or so I thought.

For some reason that I can no longer recall, I had removed the spindle nuts from both sides of the rear axle. It may have been to grease the bearings. The recommended foot pounds of pressure to retighten the spindle nuts exceeded the settings on my torque wrench. Sadly, I decided to "play it by ear."

The wisdom of Bro. Jackie's decision for me to find my own ministry, separate from his, would clearly be illustrated when he and I made a trip together in the Volkswagen to visit a hospital in Birmingham, Alabama.

We spoke and prayed with one of our church members in the hospital. We were returning to the church. We were both talking about the smoothness of the ride.

We were just south of Cullman, Alabama, on Interstate Highway 65. We were moving at a brisk 70 miles per hour when, suddenly, we felt a bump. Bro. Jackie saw a tire as it rolled past us at high speed on his side of the car. He immediately knew what had happened — the wheel had come off.

Since I was driving, he knew that he was at my mercy. He knew what to do. Or, rather, he knew what *not* to do. He started shouting, "Don't hit the brakes! Don't hit the brakes!" And he *kept on* saying it.

Finally, after about a quarter of a mile, I glanced over in his direction. I said, calmly, "I'm *not* going to hit the brakes. But may I *please* let off of the gas?"

143

Restore the Balance

Like many, if not most, rural churches, Pleasant Grove suffered from a church disease known as "koinonitis." "C. Peter Wagner, a missiologist and best-selling author, is credited with coining the term."[79] It is:

> *An introverted attitude on the part of a church such that its members devote attention to their existing relationships with each other instead of engaging in evangelism and other means of inviting new people into their congregation.*[80]

In other words, prior to Bro. Jackie's entrance onto the scene, the members of Pleasant Grove were *inwardly* focused rather than *outwardly* focused.

One of the former pastors had inadvertently raised the expectations of the members in

---

[79] http://www.dictionaryofchristianese.com/koinonia-koinonia-group-koinonitis, site visited on 2/22/2014.

[80] Ibid.

that regard. He truly loved the people. He was the quintessential *pastor*. He made a regular practice of being present at all church member surgeries. And, if that had not been enough, he would also drive patients and their family members to the hospital in his own personal car, using his own gasoline. He would wait with the family members until the surgery was finished. He would then give everyone a ride back home.

Bro. Jackie, on the other hand, would arrive at the hospital in time to have prayer with the patient before he or she went in for surgery. He stayed in the waiting room with the family members until the surgeon came out to tell the results. He then left and was thus enabled to go and make other visits.

Tip the Scales

Bro. Jackie was, without a doubt, a very complex man. As I have said, Bro. Jackie was "neither fish nor fowl." I would classify Bro.

Jackie as a composite of the best qualities of both the shepherd *and* the rancher. Whereas he would be unable, by virtue of the sheer numbers of people, to always be a pastor and would often need to revert to being a rancher, those times were extremely rare.

At first glance, his ministry would have looked something like this:

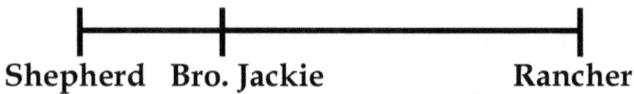

```
|———————————|——————————————————————|
Shepherd   Bro. Jackie              Rancher
```

But, again, Bro. Jackie was a complex man. He made so many visits to *non*-church members that several of us began to think that he and his gold Volkswagen Beetle had been cloned. You would see him going in one direction. A few minutes later, you would see him going back in another.

A more accurate portrayal of his style of leadership may have been like this:

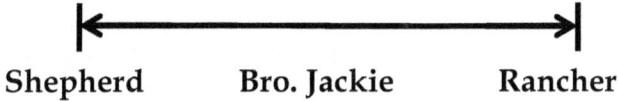

|←————————————————→|

Shepherd   **Bro. Jackie**   **Rancher**

He was an unrivaled shepherd/rancher. What could go wrong with that?

As you may know, sheepherders and ranchers have traditionally experienced difficulties in getting along, not the least of which has been the control and utilization of limited natural resources. As a result:

> *The burgeoning cattle industry [in New Mexico] was the main development of the late 19th century, and bloody battles often were fought between cattle and sheep ranchers and large and small landowners in a series of range wars.*[81]

---

[81] "New Mexico." Encyclopædia Britannica. Encyclopædia Britannica Multimedia Edition. Chicago: Encyclopædia Britannica, 2011.

Balancing the two roles obviously caused Bro. Jackie a great deal of internal conflict. His attempts to single-handedly fulfill both functions, to become a Superpastor, began to deplete his "resources" at an alarming rate.

Set the Stage

James Emery White, the founding and senior pastor of Mecklenburg Community Church in Charlotte, North Carolina, stated:

> *Shepherds are oriented toward providing primary care to their sheep. They are the ones in the trenches with coffees and funerals, discipling and weddings, one-on-ones and late-night calls. They are not usually leaders as much as chaplains.*[82]

On the other hand:

> *Ranchers are oriented toward ensuring that their sheep are properly cared for. They are leaders and visionaries, mobilizers and*

---

[82] http://www.crosswalk.com/blogs/dr-james-emery-white/the-shepherd-rancher-divide.html, site visited on 2/22/2014.

catalyzers, inspirers and motivators, change-agents and provocateurs.[83]

Bro. Jackie was not the consummate shepherd. Neither was he the conventional rancher, *in spite of* the burgeoning membership of Pleasant Grove Baptist church.

He literally sacrificed his health in order to set the stage for the transformation of the church. He was transitioning Pleasant Grove Baptist church from a "shepherd" model to a "rancher" model.

When a concerned staff member or fellow pastor would express concern for Bro. Jackie's personal well-being, he would simply shrug his shoulders and say, "You have to be willing to *pay the price* if you want to grow a great church." As you well know, he paid it—and he *kept on* paying it!

---

[83] Ibid.

You might ask, "How did he survive? How did he continue working so tirelessly for so many years?"

Thankfully, at some point, Bro. Jackie had discovered the Apostle Paul's secret:

> *For all things are for your sakes, that the abundant grace might through the thanksgiving of many redound to the glory of God. For which cause we faint not; but **though our outward man perish, yet the inward man is renewed day by day.** [Emphasis mine] For our light affliction, which is but for a moment, worketh for us a far more exceeding and eternal weight of glory; while we look not at the things which are seen, but at the things which are not seen: for the things which are seen are temporal; but the things which are not seen are eternal.*[84]

Find the Strength

Bro. Jackie's hero was, unquestionably, Jack Hyles, pastor of the First Baptist Church in Hammond, Indiana. Bro. Jackie frequently

---

[84] 2 Corinthians 4:15-18.

listened to Dr. Hyles' sermons, and was a member of his tapes-of-the-month club.

Bro. Jackie's all-time favorite message by Dr. Hyles' was entitled, "Fresh Oil."[85] The premise of "Fresh Oil" was the anointing of David, on three separate occasions, to be king over Israel. Each successive anointing was to prepare David to be in charge of "something bigger" than he had been before.

Bro. Jackie loved this! He knew that, as Pleasant Grove continued to grow, he would need more of God's power to lead the people. He would need many anointings with the "fresh oil" of God's Holy Spirit. This understanding helped him to achieve the balance he so desperately needed in order to "keep on keeping on."

---

[85] You can view this sermon in its entirety at: http://www.youtube.com/watch?v=0YtfEF0DKLE

Increase the Giving[86]

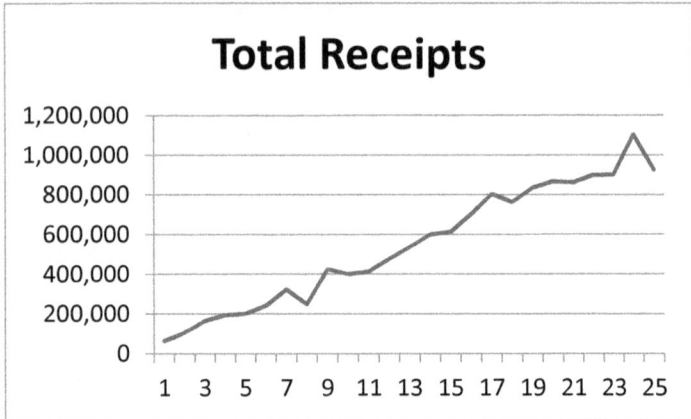

Total Receipts

As you can see by the graph[87] (above),
total receipts for Pleasant Grove Baptist Church
grew from $65,546.00 when Bro. Jackie started as
the pastor in 1980, to a high of $1,102,034.00 in
2003, a year before he retired. For you
mathematically challenged folks, that was a
whopping 1,681%!

---

[86] See Appendix D.
[87] See also Appendix D.

Jackie Shelton
His Personal Example

Bro. Jackie learned one of the greatest lessons in trusting God with his finances while working as a buyer and part owner of the Sivley Cotton Company in Hartselle, Alabama. He had a long record of success, buying and selling cotton futures in a highly volatile market.

What is high volatility? According to Chuck Kowalski, a commodities broker, an analyst and a private trader for nearly 15 years:

> *High volatility signals that a market has a higher potential for large moves. That is exactly what a trend follower wants to see. Volatility also means you have to be more diligent when you are managing the risk of your commodity trades. Traders can often get caught up in the frenzy of a fast market and let one or two bad trades wreck their portfolio.*[88]

---

[88] http://commodities.about.com/od/managingyourportfolio/a/commodity-trading-volatility.htm, site visited on 2/27/2014.

153

Bro. Jackie was so successful that he began to bargain with God: "I can pastor one of these small churches in the Moulton area. Just let me keep my job in the cotton business." That decision, he would later say, would be a mistake.

He encountered a major problem. He had bought cotton from some of the farmers at a low price just before the market price began to move up dramatically. Sivley Cotton stood to make a sizable profit.

The farmers, however, were refusing to honor their contracts. They would not sell their crop to him at the agreed upon price. His buyers in Memphis, Tennessee, expected him to be able to deliver the cotton to *them* at *their* agreed upon price. Both his integrity and his reputation were both at stake. Bro. Jackie was caught between the proverbial "rock and a hard place."

As a result, Bro. Jackie was faced with the very real possibility that the Sivley Cotton

Company could go bankrupt. He knew that, ultimately, he would be the one that had been responsible.

He prayed. And then he prayed some more. And then he surrendered. He said, "Lord, I know you want me to go to the seminary. I know you want me to get out of the cotton business. And I will. But I can't leave my partners in this condition. *Please* show me what to do."

God *did* show Bro. Jackie what to do. He followed the Lord's leadership, and it worked! The Sivley Company, rather than *losing* money that year, made a modest *gain*!

When Bro. Jackie showed his calculations to the company's accountant, the man was amazed. He added up the numbers. He double-checked his figures. He scratched his head. He shook his head vigorously from side to side. He shrugged his shoulders. Finally, he replied,

"The Sivley Cotton Company should be going out of business. There is *no way* that you could have been able to do this. With the circumstances that you were dealing with, you could not have hoped to break even this year. I can see what you did. What you have done is perfectly ethical and legal, but quite improbable. On paper, you have *lost* money. In spite of that, you have managed to make a profit!"

Bro. Jackie, on the other hand, knew exactly how it had worked. He knew that it had been the Lord. He knew that he could always trust in the Lord to provide for him *as long as* he was faithful to obey Him in the area of his finances.

Before coming to Pleasant Grove, Bro. Jackie had already established a record of lavish giving as a pastor. When he had accepted the call to Steep Hollow Baptist Church and had preached his first message as pastor there, the treasurer handed him a check in the amount of $75.00.

The next Sunday, Bro. Jackie deposited his personal check for $125.00 into the offering plate. Again, he was paid $75.00.

On the third Sunday, he gave his customary $125.00 with a return of only $75.00.

That night, the treasurer and the other members of the finance committee asked him to meet with them. The treasurer said, "Do you realize that you are giving more to the church each week than we are paying you to be our pastor?"

Bro. Jackie replied, "I am just giving what the Lord told me to give."

Bro. Jackie was dismissed from the meeting. The treasurer and members of the committee debated together for a few minutes. When the treasurer invited Bro. Jackie to come back into the room, he cheerfully announced,

"We have just voted to give you a raise — you are now making $200.00 a week!"

Bro. Jackie frequently reminded the members of Pleasant Grove that he was not only giving *sacrificially*, but he was also giving *half of his income* back to the church! And he did.

How do I know? Every year at tax time, he would tell me about his dilemma:

> *The I.R.S. won't allow me to deduct all of my charitable deductions — they go over the limit. I can't claim the rest. And this Self-Employment tax[89] is killing me!*

Bro. Jackie also made it a regular practice to leave his tithing check with the church before going on a vacation. He would tell the church members from the pulpit, "I get a paid vacation every year, and so do most of you."

---

[89] Preachers are considered to be self-employed for income tax purchases. That means they pay 100% of their Social Security and Medicare Taxes, or roughly 15.3% of their income; the employer makes no contribution on their behalf.

Waving a check in his hand, he would continue, "The work of Pleasant Grove Baptist Church doesn't stop when you or I go on vacation. So here is my check for the two weeks that I will be gone. I'm giving it now so that I won't forget to give it when I come back" (as if that would *ever* have happened).

I often wondered, "Since Bro. Jackie knows so much about the Bible, has he not read Jesus' words in Matthew 6:1-4?"

> *Take heed that ye do not your alms before men, to be seen of them: otherwise ye have no reward of your Father which is in heaven. Therefore when thou doest thine alms, do not sound a trumpet before thee, as the hypocrites do in the synagogues and in the streets, **that they may have glory of men. Verily I say unto you, "They have their reward** [emphasis mine]." But when thou doest alms, let not thy left hand know what thy right hand doeth: that thine alms may be in secret: and thy Father which seeth in secret himself shall reward thee openly.*

The key conditional phrase is found in verse two: "that they may have glory of men." The actual Greek wording is, "οπωσ δοξασθωσιν υπο των ανθρωπων."

A direct rendering of the Greek words would be, "that they might, at that point in time, be passively praised, extolled, magnified, and celebrated by human beings, whether male or female."

And don't forget Jesus' story about the widow:

> And he looked up, and saw the rich men casting their gifts into the treasury. And he saw also a certain poor widow casting in thither two mites. And he said, "Of a truth I say unto you, that this poor widow hath cast in more than they all: for all these have of their abundance cast in unto the offerings of God: but she of her penury hath cast in all the living that she had."[90]

---

[90] Luke 24:1-4.

Was Bro. Jackie guilty of *that*? Was he intentionally disobeying the Word of God? Did he desire the praises of the people? Was he, in essence, attempting to impress us?

In the words of Romans 6:2, "God forbid." Or a more accurate interpretation: "May it never become!" So why did he tell us?

I believe the answer may be found in a story related by a man named Sammy Gilbreath, at a conference I attended a few years ago. Dr. Gilbreath, director of the Office of Evangelism for the Alabama State Board of Missions, formerly served as pastor of Highland Baptist Church in Florence, Alabama. He said:

"Our church had constructed a gymnasium. We were using that building to reach unchurched kids with the Gospel. We had a lot of children coming to play basketball. That gave us the opportunity to witness to them."

"One night, in a church business meeting, one of the members rose to his feet. He said, 'Brother Sammy, I gave $10,000.00 toward building the new gymnasium. My grandson is a *member* of this church, and is on one of the basketball teams. He rarely gets to play. Oh! And did I mention that I gave $10,000.00 when we built it? Well, I did!'"

He continued, "We now have all of these kids that aren't even church members that are getting to play, while grandson sits on the bench. And I don't appreciate it. I gave $10,000.00, and I want him to be allowed to play!"

Sammy allowed the man to finish speaking—to "run out of steam." And then he replied, "Brother, I gave *$20,000.00*. Now sit down, and shut up!"

Bro. Jackie's purpose for reminding us about his giving, I believe, was twofold. First, a pastor that gives sacrificially can be extremely influential in establishing the direction for his church. He can be infinitely *more* influential when the church members know *how much* he gives. Believe me when I say that, in Bro. Jackie's case, "We knew." Whenever his vision for the church required a substantial monetary outlay[91], we also *knew* that his decision would cost him personally far more than it had any one of us.

Second, he raised the level of expectation for the rest of us. For years I had personally struggled with the question, "Should I tithe on the gross (total income) or the net (income after taxes)."

After working with Bro. Jackie, I immediately chose the former. When I became a mission pastor in Ohio, I chose to raise my

---

[91] For instance, we spent $1.2 for the new auditorium. We paid it off within around 3 years.

personal bar even higher: I began giving *20%* of my income to the church.

His Sacrifice

Bro. Jackie had a sizable bank account when he left his job in the cotton business in Hartselle, Alabama. The amount was in excess of $100,000.00! He intended to use the money for his family's living expenses during his seminary years. God, however, had a different plan.

As Bro. Jackie was praying, he felt that the Lord was leading him to "give the money away." He questioned the wisdom of this action. But the Lord continued to prompt him with the thought, "Are you going to trust in your bank account, or will you trust in Me to take care of your needs?" That settled it. He gave the money away. He and his family were now totally dependent upon the Lord.

The Lord would not fail him. He would open a door of ministry for Jackie in a most unexpected way.

His Openness

Many of your larger, "citified" churches are no longer printing monthly financial statements for their members. Church members are allowed to come to the church to view the financial information if they are interested. Other churches still distribute financial statements, but the items are placed in broad categories—staff salaries, utilities, missions, etc.

At Pleasant Grove Baptist Church, we received a financial statement *every* month. And we *always* had line-item statements. We knew every check number, to whom those checks had been written, and the exact amount, to the penny, of each and every check.

Janet Britton, our church treasurer, would bring a printout of the financial statement to the church office on the mornings of each business meeting. Bro. Jackie and I would each receive a copy. I would take a highlighter to make note of what I considered to be the "hot spots"— unusually large dollar amounts or questionable recipients of the various checks.

Bro. Jackie and I would meet that afternoon to hash through the entire document so that he would be able to answer any question that might arise in the meeting. He would then take any item or items that we could not identify and call Janet for clarification.

Why did Bro. Jackie go to all of that trouble? Because he genuinely believed in the value of transparency. He also knew that some of the regular attenders would ask at least one question before the business meeting was over.

He would always finish his public review of the financial statement with these words: "If you have any other questions about any of these

166

expenses, just come by the church office and I will try to answer them. If I don't know the answer, I will find out."

His Dignity

One particular year, Pleasant Grove hosted a Christmas party for the kids that were coming to the church through our van ministry. I wanted to offer the children some small items as gifts. I informed Bro. Jackie, "I think I will go to some of the local restaurants and businesses — you know, like McDonald's™ — to ask for some donations."

Bro. Jackie quickly responded, "Let's not do that. The people of Moulton think that churches are always going around with their hands out, asking for something. We can afford to buy gifts for the children. I would rather that you would go to the store and buy whatever you need."

He continued, "A church like Pleasant Grove that has taken a clear stand on the Gospel already has enough negative press in the community. We don't need to make the problem any worse by 'begging for alms'[92] when we can afford to buy anything we need."

He was, obviously, concerned about the church's reputation in the community; he was also concerned about his own. He knew that a rural pastor will have the reputation of being either a giver or a taker. *Everyone* knew. Bro. Jackie was a giver.

His Beneficence

During the time my family and I served at the mission church in Toledo, Ohio, we made a return visit to Pleasant Grove. I was given the opportunity to share what God had been doing in our church.

---

[92] Acts 3:2.

When I had finished speaking, Bro. Jackie walked up to the podium. He said, "We all love Bro. Scott, Diane, Michael, Kelly, and Susanna. They have made a great sacrifice by going to Ohio to serve the Lord. I believe we ought to take up a special offering for them."

He reached deeply into his own pocket. He produced a $100 bill. He said, "I am giving $100.00 toward this offering. Let's honor God and Bro. Scott's sacrifice with our gifts."

Following his example, the people were extremely generous. What a benevolent man of God!

Share the Load

"Sharing the Load" was, perhaps, the last technique that Bro. Jackie had been able to master. For many years, he had literally been carrying the pastoral load all by himself. And, I believe, that had been by design.

When I had started working with Bro. Jackie in 1984, he rarely asked me to make any hospital visits. On those rare occasions when he did, he had already previously visited with the patients.

Why? As a rural pastor, he knew that he could have sent the deacons, other staff members, and Sunday school teachers to visit in the hospitals *in his stead*. But he also knew that simply wouldn't work. Like it or not, rural church members expect their *pastor* to visit them when they are sick. If he doesn't, the grapevine, "an informal person-to-person means of circulating information or gossip[93]," will flourish!

The rural pastor, for years, may go faithfully to all of the hospitals. It may seem unreasonable, but the first time the rural pastor

---

[93] MERRIAM-WEBSTER'S COLLEGIATE DICTIONARY AND THESAURUS, DELUXE AUDIO EDITION®.

neglects to visit even one member, the word will begin to spread throughout the community, "Our pastor *never* visits people when they are in the hospital." And that rumor will *never* go away.

Bro. Jackie, as has been said, knew that hospital visitation was an indelible part of the pastor's *unwritten* job description. Because we, at any given time, had many members in the hospital, he learned the necessity of making brief visits. He told me, "I have learned the secret of making my hospital visits early in the morning. Many times, when I arrive, the patients are asleep. And that's good. They don't feel like talking when they first wake up. I pray for them and then leave."

His Solution

A year or so after my family and I had gone to the mission church in Toledo, Ohio, Bro. Jackie asked Neil Carter to become his new associate pastor. Neil, a native north Alabamian, had previously been the pastor of Providence Baptist Church in Hatton, Alabama,[94] for several years.

I believe that the primary reason he hired Neil was to assist him in the area of his pastoral ministries. Bro. Jackie likely thought "Since Neil had already been a pastor (unlike me—I had been a recent seminary graduate before working at Pleasant Grove), the people would also accept him as a pastor. They would allow him to visit them in the hospitals, preach their funerals, and perform their weddings."[95]

Bro. Jackie had solved the dilemma. No one would be able to complain. A *pastor* would still be visiting them when they were in the hospital, *another* pastor, a *different* pastor. And,

---

[94] A church in our same local association.

[95] Bro. Jackie told me, "I would rather preach at a funeral than perform a wedding." I asked, "Why?" He said, "They don't come back on you!"

as far as I could tell when I returned to Pleasant Grove in 1992, his plan had worked.

As a result, Neil made frequent visits to the hospital. He assisted Bro. Jackie with numerous funerals. He and his wife, Debbie, also assumed many of the responsibilities of working with the senior adults. In so doing, they were able to give Bro. Jackie the valuable time that he needed to fulfill his other pursuits in the church.

After nearly thirty years, Neil still serves at Pleasant Grove. He has also been asked to assist in a majority of the funerals since Jackie's retirement. Additionally, he was asked by the family members to participate in Bro. Jackie's funeral service in 2013.

On a Lighter Note

Rather than hiring another pastor to help him with hospital visitation, Bro. Jackie *could* have adopted Jerry Vine's policy at East Rome

Baptist Church in Rome, Georgia. Apparently, East Rome Baptist had grown so large so quickly that Dr. Vines was unable to visit all of the sick folks in the hospital.

As a result, the deacons became the primary visitors to the hospitals from the church. Whenever one of the deacons would discover that a church member was in a serious or life-threatening condition, he would notify Dr. Vines.

The fact that Dr. Vines would only visit the terminal or near-terminal patients eventually became widely known to the members of East Rome Baptist Church. They began dreading the possibility of a visit from their pastor. In response to his visit, one person allegedly shouted, "Oh, no! Am I that sick?"

The members of Pleasant Grove (and nonmembers) had no such concerns. They knew that when they were in the hospital, whether for minor illnesses or major surgeries, one of their pastors would be coming for a visit.

Distinguish Yourself

Bro. Jackie worked long hours, and he worked extremely hard. But you rarely saw him participate in a church work day. He would come to the site. He would pray for us. But, since he would typically be wearing a dress shirt and khaki pants, none of us expected him to be digging any holes! He was occasionally even criticized for not helping.

This behavior didn't make sense to any of us. We all knew that he kept his car clean and his yard well-maintained. He knew how to work. In fact, he worked longer hours than any other man in the church.

I now realize that he was in the process of distinguishing himself as the pastor of the church. That objective also explained why he was constantly reminding the people of Pleasant

Grove about his prayer life and his record of giving.

King Solomon, in his dedication of the Temple, said:

> *But will God indeed dwell on the earth? Behold, the heaven and heaven of heavens cannot contain thee; how much less this house that I have builded?*[96]

Solomon recognized the transcendence of God—that God is greater than His creation.

Mind you, Bro. Jackie did not have a God-complex. He did, however, understand the danger of becoming "just one of the folks." He knew that, to command respect, he would need to distinguish himself from his church members.

A Personal Note

I wish that I had learned this valuable lesson of *separation* from Bro. Jackie. Sadly, I did not.

---

[96] 1 Kings 8:27.

Two experiences caused me to disregard Bro. Jackie's example. First, I read a book entitled <u>Transitioning</u>[97] several years ago. The author, Dan Southerland, is currently one of the pastors of Next Level Church in Charlotte, North Carolina. Dan stated in the book that, although he had an earned doctorate, he had chosen to remove the artificial barriers that had separated him from his members. He had given his parishioners permission to simply address him as "Dan."

Second, while attending the Mid-America Baptist Theological Seminary, I became close personal friends with one of my professors, Dr. Steve Wilkes. After I had received my Doctor of Ministry degree, he and I participated together in several foreign mission trips. I had also led a

---

[97] Dan Southerland. <u>Transitioning: Leading Your Church Through Change</u> (Grand Rapids: Zondervan Publishing Corp., 2000).

couple of groups that had been sponsored by his organization, World-Wide Church Planters.

Out of respect, I always addressed him as "Doctor" Wilkes. He stopped me. He said, "Just call me 'Wilkes."

I responded, "I can't do that. You are *Doctor* Wilkes."

He said, "I was Wilkes a long time before I became a doctor." He repeated, "So just call me 'Wilkes.'" And so I did. And I thought (and rightfully so) that he was a very down to earth, humble servant of our Lord, Jesus Christ.

Combining these two experiences, I decided to follow suit. When I arrived at my last full-time church, someone asked me, "What should we call you — *Doctor* Moore or *Brother* Scott?" I replied, "Just call me 'Scott.'" Parroting what I had heard *Doctor* Wilkes say, I continued, "I was *Scott* a long time before I was *Doctor Moore*." Some of the church members

178

were intrigued, some were impressed, and others were uncomfortable.

Shortly after my resignation from the church, my former church secretary told me that she had thought the decision to let the people call me by my first name had been a mistake. She said, "Because you wouldn't let us call you 'Doctor Moore' or, at least, 'Brother Scott,' the people didn't *respect* you. They thought you were just *one of us* [emphasis mine]."

By maintaining a degree of separation, a space between himself and the church members, Bro. Jackie was, once again, demonstrating his God-given wisdom for leading a rural church. He was, as they say, "A smart cookie."

The Spiritual Stall

Bro. Jackie was a master of what I will call the "Spiritual Stall Technique." The pastor of a church of any size will tell you that he is asked to make dozens, if not hundreds, of decisions

179

each and every day. People will come from all sides to ask, "Pastor, what do you think we should do?"

Bro. Jackie had learned, the hard way, to wait before making any major decisions. He privately related the following story to me: "A good family was regularly attending our church. The husband was a very successful business-man, and was a major supporter of our Pleasant Grove. His wife, however, didn't particularly like the church. She was constantly trying to persuade him to leave."

"One day, another church member approached me. He told me that we needed to install ceiling fans in the auditorium. He said, 'Ceiling fans will help circulate the warm air in the winter, saving us hundreds, if not thousands, of dollars in energy costs.' 'And,' he said, 'I will install them, free of charge.'" Bro. Jackie confessed, "And I agreed."

He continued, "That was just the decision that this wife had been waiting for. She said to her husband, 'You know I have a problem with my allergies. Those ceiling fans are just making it worse. We will have to leave. Please take me to another church.' And so he did."

Bro. Jackie lamented, "We lost a great church member, and I learned a valuable lesson: never allow yourself to be forced into an immediate decision. Always take the time to pray."

From that moment on, whenever anyone would press for him to make an on-the-spot decision, he would simply reply, "Let's pray about it." And the matter would be settled.

Webster has defined the word "stall" as: "to play for time," and "to hold off, divert, or delay by evasion or deception."[98] Bro. Jackie's stall was to say, "Let's pray about it."

Why did he choose those words? For a couple of reasons: first, although he knew that he *would* pray about it, he also knew that you probably *wouldn't*.

Second, when impatient people were demanding that we "do something right now" he was able to postpone the decision. Over time, the majority of people would simply give up on promoting their ideas.

Sadly, even though I was an insider, and Bro. Jackie had previously revealed his strategy to me, that didn't stop him from using it on me. On more than one occasion he said *me*, "Scott, let's pray about it."

---

[98] MERRIAM-WEBSTER'S COLLEGIATE DICTIONARY AND THESAURUS, DELUXE AUDIO EDITION®.

<u>Defend the Workers</u>

Bro. Jackie had an unwritten policy was to never fire any of his workers. In his mind, the cost of terminating an employee in a rural church must have been much higher than the cost of keeping them.

You might ask, "What led Bro. Jackie to this understanding?" For one thing, he was fiercely loyal to his people. He would occasionally tell me that someone had come to him with a complaint about my work or the work of another staff member. His response was always the same. "You need to pray for him." And, just as it had been with the elderly deacon, the matter was settled.

For another thing, during his years of service as a deacon at the Moulton Baptist Church he had observed the actions of many pastors. He had seen what *had* worked—and what had *not* worked. He had likely watched one or more of these pastors as they had made the decision to terminate an employee or to ask a volunteer to relinquish his or her position in the church. He had also seen the aftermath of those decisions.

He then followed Jesus' admonition:[99] "For which of you, intending to build a tower, sitteth not down first, and counteth the cost, whether he have sufficient to finish it?" He counted the cost. For Bro. Jackie, the cost would have simply been too high. He survived, for 24 years, in a rural church—a church in which, over the years, countless others had failed.

To illustrate this point, Bro. Jackie told me the story of the minister of music he inherited when he arrived at Steep Hollow Baptist Church. No sooner had Bro. Jackie accepted the call to the church when a man accosted him with

---

[99] Luke 14:28.

the demand, "You need to get rid of Brother 'Bike.[100]'"

Brother Jackie replied, "Why? Why do you think he needs to go?"

The man responded, "Because he is a *terrible* song leader. And he can't sing. We can do better."

I am not sure if Bro. Jackie had perfected his renowned "stall technique," or if it was simply a work in progress. But he said, at that precise moment, "Let's pray about it."

And Bro. Jackie *did* pray. The Lord led him to keep Brother "Bike" as his minister of music. Bro. Jackie told me, "And I am glad that I did. Brother 'Bike' may not have been the best song leader in the world. But he was a godly man and he loved Jesus. I couldn't have asked for a better person for the job."

---

[100] I am not sure about the spelling of the man's name.

Bro. Jackie maintained this commitment to keeping staff members when he arrived at Pleasant Grove Baptist Church. Although I worked with him for 10 of his 24 years at Pleasant Grove, he never terminated a single staff person. He never asked a teacher, a van driver, or even a cleaning person to resign. Even though, parenthetically, several of us may have deserved it!

He instinctively knew the truth contained in an article written by Pilar Ethridge, entitled, "How to Fire Church Employees." Ethridge, assistant editor of a Washington, D.C., newsletter, stated:

> *Church employees are often members of the church and can be very involved in the community. That can make it difficult to fire the employee. Breaking spiritual ties that have been interlaced with business/workplace*

ties can be hurtful and damaging to all parties involved.[101]

On one occasion, an elderly deacon had chosen to remarry after the death of his wife. The marriage, after one year, had tragically failed.

Two sides of the issue quickly emerged within the body of deacons. One group believed that the man needed to resign as a deacon, since the Bible teaches that a deacon must be "the husband of one wife."[102]

The other group felt compassion for the man. They wanted to let him remain in his capacity as a deacon.

Bro. Jackie intervened. He stepped in quickly in an effort to defuse the problem. Acknowledging the concerns of the first group, he said, "We all know what the Bible says about

---

[101] http://www.ehow.com/how_8259091_fire-church-employees.html, site visited on 2/21/2014.
[102] 1Timothy 3:2.

deacons and divorce. And we *could* ask the man to resign."

Turning his attention to the entire group, he said, "But I have an alternative. Let's let him keep his dignity. Let's allow him to become an inactive member of the deacon body."

Focusing on the second group, he said, "As an inactive deacon, he will still be a deacon, but he will no longer serve. He has already offered to become inactive. I think we should let him."

Members of the first group were not satisfied. They still wanted the man to resign. But Bro. Jackie was adamant. The deacons finally agreed. The matter was settled.

His standing policy regarding termination may have seemed, to many, to be somewhat laissez-faire. But in Bro. Jackie's mind, as has been stated, the price of letting someone go would have been much higher than the price of keeping them.

On a Lighter Note

While still a member and a deacon at Moulton Baptist Church, Bro. Jackie was asked to serve on the pulpit committee to participate in the selection of the next pastor. The committee members made arrangements to go to another church in order to hear a sermon from one of their potential candidates.

The candidate did an outstanding job. The committee members were looking forward to meeting with him after the service. Each member, in turn, was given the opportunity to ask questions of the candidate. They liked his answers.

And then someone asked, "What is the first thing you would do if we were to call you to become the pastor of our church?"

The man bluntly replied, "I would fire all of the staff."

The candidate was dismissed from the room. One of the committee members also happened to be the Minister of Music at Moulton Baptist. He said to the other members, "If this is our guy, I will just resign. He won't have to fire *me*."

In unison, the rest of the committee members replied, "He's not our guy."

This experience so impacted Bro. Jackie that he was able to describe it to me, in detail, many years later. Is it any wonder that, in all of his years as pastor of Pleasant Grove, he never terminated an employee, or that he never forced a volunteer worker to resign? [103]

---

[103] That is, to my knowledge. And I was definitely among the insiders of the church.

190

Stay Where You Are Planted

Bro. Jackie was fond of saying, "I don't need a résumé. God knows where I am." And he was right.

Bro. Jackie occasionally entertained the notion of moving away from Pleasant Grove. I believe that he came close to leaving in 1986. He told a very frightened, inexperienced young minister (me), "You may be the next pastor of Pleasant Grove Baptist Church."

My thoughts were similar to the words of David when he said, "I was glad when they said unto me, 'Let us go into the house of the LORD.'"[104] *I* was glad when *Bro. Jackie* said unto me, "I'm not going anywhere. The Lord wants me to stay here."

---

[104] Psalm 122:1.

Ride the Wave of Momentum

I believe that 1985 was a pivotal year for Pleasant Grove Baptist Church. Bro. Jackie had been struggling in his attempts to grow the church.

And then something amazing began to happen at Pleasant Grove. We baptized 96 people into the membership of the church.[105] The next year, as a result of a Junior Hill revival, we baptized 105 more. And the ball began to roll. Pleasant Grove Baptist Church began to experience a period of *significant* growth.

Why? What had made the difference? What had changed? We were now riding the wave of a phenomenon called "momentum." Regarding momentum, author and motivational speaker John C. Maxwell stated:

> *When you have no momentum, even the simplest tasks seem impossible. Small prob-*

---

[105] See Appendix B.

lems look like insurmountable obstacles. Morale becomes low. The future appears dark. An organization with no momentum is like a train at a dead stop. It's hard to get going, and even small wooden blocks on the track can keep it from going anywhere.[106]

Maxwell continued:

On the other hand, when you have momentum on your side, the future looks bright, obstacles appear small, and troubles seem inconsequential. An organization with momentum is like a train that's moving at sixty miles per hour. You could build a steel-reinforced concrete wall across the tracks, and the train would plow right through it.[107]

Momentum can be either the rural pastor's best friend or his worst nightmare. It will either work for him, or work against him.

---

[106] Maxwell, John (2012-08-28). The Law of the Big Mo: Lesson 16 from The 21 Irrefutable Laws of Leadership (Kindle Locations 104-107). Thomas Nelson. Kindle Edition.

[107] Maxwell, John. The Law of the Big Mo (Kindle Locations 107-110).

In order to grow a rural church, the *pastor* must become the initiator. Maxwell concluded:

> *It takes a leader to create momentum. Followers can catch it. Good managers are able to use it to their advantage once it has begun. Everyone can enjoy the benefits it brings. But creating momentum requires someone who has vision, can assemble a good team, and motivates others.*[108]

Bro. Jackie had accepted the responsibility of overcoming the *inertia* in his organization. What is inertia? It is:

> *A property of matter by which it remains at rest or in uniform motion in the same straight line unless acted upon by some external force; an indisposition to motion, exertion, or change.*[109]

Jackie Shelton had accepted the challenge. He had refused to follow the pack. He had refused

---

[108] Maxwell, John. <u>The Law of the Big Mo</u> (Kindle Locations 161-163).

[109] Maxwell, John. <u>The Law of the Big Mo</u> (Kindle Locations 161-163).

to accept things in his church as he had found them. He had dared to "rock the boat." He had achieved his dream. He had truly become the pastor of the "Greatest Rural Church in America!"

HIS COUNSEL

I often sought Bro. Jackie's counsel while I was pastor of the King's Road Baptist Church in Toledo, Ohio. And he was more than happy to give it.

Be Visible

Bro. Jackie said, "When you get up there (to Toledo, Ohio), you will need to make yourself visible."

I asked, "What do you mean by that?"

He replied, "For instance, instead of going through the drive-through at the bank, get out of your car and go in. Mingle with the people. Get to know them."

That made sense. He continued, "And get out in the community. Go door to door. Let people know where you are and why you are there."

On a Lighter Note

I followed Bro. Jackie's advice to visit the people in the community. Leaving from the church one Saturday morning, I drove south on King Road. I noticed a man raking leaves about three doors down from the church.

I pulled off onto the side of the road. The man dropped his rake. He approached my car. With a sour look, he asked, "May I help you?"

I replied, "No. I just wanted to introduce myself. My name is Scott Moore." I pointed in the direction of the church. I continued, "And I am the new pastor of the King's Road Baptist Church."

The man's expression became noticeably hardened. He pointed with his thumb toward a statue of Mary in front of his house. He said, sarcastically, "I guess you can tell by what you see right there that I am not a Baptist." I nodded.

And then he pointed at my car. He said, in a not-so-friendly tone, "And your car is on my grass. I would appreciate it if you would move it *right now.*"

I knew at that moment that I was no longer serving in a rural church in Moulton, Alabama. Rural people tend to be much friendlier to strangers. They would never have a problem with someone parking on their grass!

Stay Focused

After three years in Ohio, I felt the need to "force the issue" of constituting our church. I wanted to break the ties with our sponsoring church. I had discovered that our "mother" church held the title deed to our property, even though we had been making all of the payments.

I needed Bro. Jackie's wisdom. So I called him on the telephone. He related the following experience from his time at Steep Hollow to me: "The church had begun to grow. The membership had increased to the point that more buildings were needed. I approached several of the church leaders with the need. Some of the leaders pointed out that the church did not officially own the land upon which the current buildings had been erected."

"They asked, 'Why would we want to put any more money into property that we don't even own.'"

"The issue to which they were referring was the fact that the land had been donated *conditionally* to the church. Should the members of the church ever vote to disband, the land and all of its improvements would revert to the ownership of the family that had donated it. The church, therefore, didn't have clear title."

Undaunted, Bro. Jackie said, "Who cares? We need more room for the people that are coming. What difference does it make what happens to the land and the buildings if we stop growing and eventually cease to exist as a church?"

He won the day. They built the much-need educational space. And they eventually built a new auditorium and more educational space — on land that belonged to someone else.

His point was valid. We need to go about the Lord's business of reaching people. It doesn't matter who owns the property or who gets the credit. God knows. And He will reward us for a job well done.

HIS RETIREMENT AND HOMEGOING

I have already mentioned the crocheted quotation about Moses and the inefficiency of committees that was placed on Bro. Jackie's desk. Another prominent feature of his office was a picture that hung on the wall. It was a typical, tiny, white-framed church building in the middle of the woods. When someone would ask Bro. Jackie what that picture represented, he would say, "That's my dream church. That's where I am going when I retire."[110]

Bro. Jackie fulfilled that dream, but only temporarily. After his retirement in 2004, he was

---

[110] Neil Carter once said, "The only problem with Bro. Jackie going to that little church is that it will start to grow. It will become the next Pleasant Grove."

asked to serve as the pastor a small Baptist church. Although First Baptist Church of Littleville, Alabama, was not in the woods—it was on a state highway—Bro. Jackie saw the church, nonetheless, as a rural place where he could continue to serve. He was looking forward to a much-needed, slower place. And he tried.

But then the unthinkable happened—he was diagnosed with Parkinson's disease! The effects began to take their toll:

> *Parkinson's disease is a motor disorder characterized by the onset of a "pill rolling" rhythmic tremor, muscle rigidity, difficulty and slowness in movement, and stooped posture. As the disease progresses, the face of the patient becomes expressionless, the rate of swallowing is reduced, leading to drooling, and depression and* **dementia** *[emphasis mine] increase.*[111]

---

[111] "Human Disease." Encyclopædia Britannica. Encyclopædia Britannica Multimedia Edition. Chicago: Encyclopædia Britannica, 2011.

The characteristic of the disease that concerned him the most was the dementia.

I spoke with Bro. Jackie at his home in 2012. He told me that the reason he had chosen to leave the church in Littleville was that he felt that he could no longer adequately preach. He said, "I would get up there [in the pulpit] and just forget what I was going to say."

How tragic! A man renowned for his sharp mind, a man that could remember thousands of names and hundreds of Bible verses, was now suffering from this terrible affliction.

However, Bro. Jackie had no regrets. When he left this life on Tuesday, April 2, 2013, he was surrounded by the people he loved—his wife, his three boys, and his grandchildren.

According to his son, Ben, his last words were hard to understand. And then he clearly said, "All I want to do is serve the Lord."

Like the Apostle Paul, Bro. Jackie could confidently say:[112]

> *I have fought the good fight, I have finished the course, I have kept the faith; in the future there is laid up for me the crown of righteousness, which the lord, the righteous judge, will award to me on that day; and not only to me, but also to all who have loved his appearing.*

What had kept Jackie Shelton going all of those years? What had been his motivation? Didn't he ever want to quit? I'm sure that he did. Did he ever want to slow down? Certainly.

But the fact is — he didn't. The reason? Bro. Jackie knew that, one day, he would stand before his Lord, Jesus Christ.[113] He wanted to hear Him say:

> *Well done, thou good and faithful servant: thou hast been faithful over a few things, I*

---

[112] 2 Timothy 4:7-8.

[113] That day, for him, was Tuesday, April 2, 2013.

will make thee ruler over many things: enter thou into the joy of thy lord.[114]

Did Bro. Jackie hear those words on that fateful day? You be the judge. Or, rather, why don't we let *Jesus* be the judge. Just between you and me, is there any doubt?

---

[114] Matthew 25:21.

HIS PROPHET'S MANTLE

The following is the story of Elijah and Elisha[115]:

When they had crossed, Elijah said to Elisha, "Tell me, what can I do for you before I am taken from you?" "Let me inherit a double portion of your spirit," Elisha replied. "You have asked a difficult thing," Elijah said, "yet if you see me when I am taken from you, it will be yours — otherwise not." As they were walking along and talking together, suddenly a chariot of fire and horses of fire appeared and separated the two of them, and Elijah went up to heaven in a whirlwind. Elisha saw this and cried out, "My father! My father! The chariots and horsemen of Israel!" And Elisha saw him no more. Then he took hold of his own clothes and tore them apart. He picked up the cloak that had fallen from

---

[115] 2 Kings 2:9-15.

Elijah and went back and stood on the bank of the Jordan. Then he took the cloak that had fallen from him and struck the water with it. "Where now is the LORD, the God of Elijah?" he asked. When he struck the water, it divided to the right and to the left, and he crossed over. The company of the prophets from Jericho, who were watching, said, "The spirit of Elijah is resting on Elisha." And they went to meet him and bowed to the ground before him.

Will you join with me in assuming the prophet's mantle? Will you help to continue the work in rural churches that Bro. Jackie has left for us to do?

It's up to you. You must choose. But choose quickly. Remember the words of our Savior? He said, "I must work the works of him that sent me, while it is day: the night cometh, when no man can work."[116]

---

[116] John 9:4.

A FINAL WORD

or "spiritual" reasons, since my return to Alabama in 1992, I have rejected many of the principles that I have delineated in this book. I haven't always agreed with Bro. Jackie. I haven't always approved of his methods. But, as I have discovered over the years, and sadly by experience, *I* had the right to be wrong!

The words of the old Chinese proverb still ring true today, "The wise man learns from the mistakes of others, the fool learns only from his own." Be wise. You will immediately embrace some of what you read in this book. Other parts of the book may, at first, cause you to wonder about their effectiveness.

Read this book. And then read it again. Share it with a friend. Absorb it. Make it a part of your overall strategy for leading your church.

As Bro. Jackie said to me nearly thirty years ago, "You could be the next pastor of the "Greatest Rural Church in America."

APPENDICES

Appendix A
Sunday school Enrollment and Attendance

Year	Average Sunday school Attendance	Sunday school Enrollment	Attendance/ Enrollment (Percentage)
1980	153	263	58%
1981	194	371	52%
1982	257	533	48%
1983	288	620	46%
1984	293	677	43%
1985	326	874	37%
1986	345	1027	34%
1987	349	1140	31%

1988	361	1233	29%
1989	374	1328	30%
1990	404	1447	28%
1991	419	1570	27%
1992	431	1756	25%
1993	435	1863	23%
1994	438	1983	22%
1995	453	2121	21%
1996	482	2249	21%
1997	491	2344	21%
1998	510	2475	21%
1999	519	2564	20%
2000	519	2673	19%
2001	508	2769	18%
2002	507	2492	20%
2003	510	2615	20%
2004	516	2667	19%

Appendix B
Discipleship Training Attendance

Year	Average Attendance
1980	74
1981	112
1982	
1983	
1984	
1985	
1986	213
1987	216
1988	218
1989	224
1990	234
1991	244
1992	246
1993	282

Appendix C
Total Baptisms

Year	Baptisms	Junior Hill Decisions
1980	3	
1981	41	
1982	88	
1983	49	
1984	51	
1985	96	
1986	105	41
1987	56	
1988	81	
1989	64	24
1990	71	
1991	70	
1992	74	
1993	96	55

1994	61	
1995	76	
1996	42	
1997	81	64
1998	86	
1999	61	
2000	108	50
2001	65	
2002	44	
2003	36	
2004	48	
Totals	1653	234

Appendix D
Total Receipts

Year	Total Receipts
1980	$65,546.00
1981	$164,295.00
1982	$164,295.00
1983	$194,295.00
1984	$201,175.00
1985	$241,515.00
1986	$323,715.00
1987	$248,575.00
1988	$424,975.00
1989	$401,086.00
1990	$411,625.00
1991	$476,345.00
1992	$535,725.00
1993	$601,125.00
1994	$612,824.00
1995	$704,206.00

1996	$803,852.00
1997	$764,396.00
1998	$835,209.00
1999	$867,150.00
2000	$861,999.00
2001	$899,820.00
2002	$901,410.00
2003	$1,102,034.00
2004	$925,766.00
Totals	$13,732,958.00

BIBLIOGRAPHY

Books

Francis, David. The 5-Step Formula for Sunday
    school Growth (Nashville: LifeWay Press,
    2005).

Hunt, Johnny M. Building Your Leadership
    Résumé: Developing the Legacy that Will
    Outlast You (Nashville: Broadman and
    Holman Publishing Group, 2003).

Maxwell, John (2012-08-28). The Law of the Big
    Mo: Lesson 16 from The 21 Irrefutable
    Laws of Leadership (Kindle Locations
    104-107). Thomas Nelson. Kindle Edition.

McLemore, Dusty. Gambling with Eternity: The
    Loser Wins (Athens, AL: LLBC
    Publishing, 2014).

MERRIAM-WEBSTER'S COLLEGIATE
DICTIONARY AND THESAURUS,
DELUXE AUDIO EDITION®, Version
2.5, Copyright © Merriam-
Webster, Incorporated, 47 Federal Street,
P.O. Box 28l, Springfield, MA 01102.

<u>Pleasant Grove Baptist Church Directory</u>
(Galion, OH: United Church Directories,
circa 2003)

Richards, Lawrence O. <u>Youth Ministry</u> (Grand
Rapids: Zondervan Publishing Corp.,
1972).

Southerland, Dan. <u>Transitioning: Leading Your
Church Through Change</u> (Grand Rapids:
Zondervan Publishing Corp., 2000).

Encyclopedia Articles

"Human Disease." <u>Encyclopædia Britannica</u>.
<u>Encyclopædia Britannica Multimedia
Edition</u>. Chicago: Encyclopædia
Britannica, 2011.

"New Mexico." Encyclopædia Britannica. <u>Encyclopædia Britannica Multimedia Edition</u>. Chicago: Encyclopædia Britannica, 2011.

Newspapers

"Moulton-area Church Marks 150 Years with Reflections of Past, Vision for Future." <u>The Alabama Baptist</u>. 7 December 2006.

"Wren Pastor Retires after 23 Growing Years." <u>The Alabama Baptist</u>. 24 June 2004.

Websites

http://50alive.com/gpage2.html, site visited on 2/25/2014.

http://www.brainyquote.com/quotes/quotes/h/harrystru109615.html, site visited on 3/2/2014.

http://commodities.about.com/od/managingyourportfolio/a/commodity-trading-volatility.htm, site visited on 2/27/2014.

http://www.city-data.com/city/Poplarville-Mississippi.html, site visited on 2/19/2014/

http://www.crosswalk.com/blogs/dr-james-emery-white/the-shepherd-rancher-divide.html, site visited on 2/22/2014.

http://www.dictionaryofchristianese.com/koinonia-koinonia-group-koinonitis, site visited on 2/22/2014.

http://www.ehow.com/how_8259091_fire-church-employees.html, site visited on 2/21/2014.

http://eodinfo.tamu.edu/media/80952/generations.pdf, site visited on 2/25/2014/

http://www.foxnews.com/opinion/2012/06/03/obesity-epidemic-in-america-churches/, site visited on 3/13/2014.

http://going.imb.org/3yrsormore/details.asp?toryID=7441&LanguageID=1709, site visited on 3/10/2014,

http://jasonbhuffman.wordpress.com/2011/02/14/things-to-know-about-rural-church-ministry/, site visited on 2/21/2014.

http://www.johnmaxwell.com/blog/the-law-
of-the-lid, site visited on 2/20/2014.

http://www.lifeway.com/Product/enrollment-
card-permanent-record-of-progress-form-
10-P001149148

http://www.mabts.edu/academics/get-know-
our-faculty/faculty-bios/dr-david-
skinner, site visited on 2/25/2014.

http://www.mapquest.com/#d841b86fd8999b2
f868a156c, site visited on 2/20/2014.

http://www.mapquest.com/#b15628d9b6fb362
1bf015928, site visited on 2/20/2014.

http://www.obitsforlife.com/obituary/617850/
Shelton-Hilda.php, site visited on
3/5/2014.

http://www.obitsforlife.com/obituary685298/S
helton--Jackie-.php, site visited on
2/18/2014.

http://www.poplarville.net, site visited on
2/19/2014.

http://www.searchquotes.com/quotation/If_you_always_do_what_you%27ve_always_done%2C_you%27ll_always_get_what_you_always_got%2C_and_you%27ll_always_f/288393/, site visited on 3/2/2014.

http://www.sschool.com/content/adultstart.htm, site visited on 3/13/2014.

http://texasbaptists.org/files/2012/10/Sunday-School-Enrollment.pdf, site visited on 2/20/2014.

http://www.trinityfulton.com/importance-of-sunday-school-enrollment, site visited on 2/21/2014.

https://twitter.com/DaveRamsey/status/440136594343739394, site visited on 3/2/2014.

http://www.urbandictionary.com/define.php?term=bless+your+heart, site visited on 3/2/2014.

http://www.urbandictionary.com/define.php?term=rubber+necking, site visited on 2/28/2014.

W. Scott Moore

During a ministerial career of more than three decades, Christian author W. Scott Moore, Bachelor of Business Administration, Master of Divinity, Doctor of Ministry, has served for ten of those years with Jackie Shelton as his bus minister, children's pastor, youth minister, and associate pastor. He is currently the senior pastor of a rural church in north Alabama.